THE ANC UNDERGROUND IN SOUTH AFRICA, 1950–1976

THE ANC UNDERGROUND

IN SOUTH AFRICA,

1950–1976

Raymond Suttner

FIRST**FORUM**PRESS

A DIVISION OF LYNNE RIENNER PUBLISHERS, INC. • BOULDER & LONDON

Published in the United States of America in 2009 by
FirstForumPress
A division of Lynne Rienner Publishers, Inc.
1800 30th Street, Boulder, Colorado 80301
www.firstforumpress.com

and in the United Kingdom by
FirstForumPress
A division of Lynne Rienner Publishers, Inc.
3 Henrietta Street, Covent Garden, London WC2E 8LU

First published by Jacana Media (Pty) Ltd. in 2008

Library of Congress Cataloging-in-Publication Data
Suttner, Raymond.
The ANC underground in South Africa, 1950–1976 / by Raymond Suttner.
  Includes index.
  ISBN 978-1-935049-13-5 (hardcover: alk. paper)
  1. African National Congress—History. 2. South Africa—Politics and
government—20th century. 3. South Africa—History. I. Title.
JQ1998.A4S874 2009
322.4'2096809045—dc22   2009009408

British Cataloguing in Publication Data
A Cataloguing in Publication record for this book
is available from the British Library.

Printed and bound in the United States of America

5 4 3 2 1

*To all those whose story
has yet to be told*

CONTENTS

ACKNOWLEDGMENTS

This work was started around 2000, although it was part of a wider range of research projects, completed in various ways or still in progress. The costs for the interviews conducted in South Africa were met by generous funding from the Nordic Africa Institute through the Swedish Agency for Development and Cooperation (SIDA), from 2001 to 2005. I am grateful to the then Institute Director, Lennart Wohlgemuth, and the Director of Research, Henning Melber, for steering this process.

During this period I was based at the Centre for Policy Studies, which provided a congenial environment. I am indebted to Steven Friedman, head at the time, for inviting me and for continuing to be a friend and scholar with whom I can always share ideas. While at the Centre I received considerable support from staff, in particular Claire Kruger, Martin Ngobeni, Soneni Ncube, Rangena Mogale, Portia Santho and Stella Tshona, who collected library books and copied large documents for me, and helped in countless other ways.

From 2003 I have also been associated in various capacities with the University of South Africa. Initially I was based in the History Department on a part-time basis and, from late 2006, full-time in the School for Graduate Studies. I have had the good fortune to work under Greg Cuthbertson most of this time; it has been a relationship from which I have benefited greatly and a friendship on which I can rely. In addition, the sourcing skills of Mary-Lynn Suttie often uncovered works in the Unisa library that opened new areas of inquiry.

At various points I have drawn on the encouragement and advice of others, like Tom Lodge, Eddie Webster and Sobizana Mngqikana.

Phil Bonner and Vladimir Shubin provided careful comments on a previous version of this work. From the early days of the research, when its direction was not clear, I have been in regular correspondence with

Shubin, Irina Filatova, Gail Gerhart and Tom Karis. They all provided unstinting support and, while often disagreeing with me, nevertheless ensured that I was aware of sources that I might not otherwise have used to test my arguments thoroughly.

I thank Maggie Davey for urging me to submit the work to Jacana as the principal publisher. That has meant dealing with Russell Martin and Priscilla Hall, who helped make the work more readable.

My wife, Nomboniso Gasa, was herself an underground worker and consequently was able to provide insights that enriched or tested what I have written and contributed substantially to the gendered nature of this work.

—R. S.

1

INTRODUCTION

This work started as a much broader project examining the cultures of the African National Congress (ANC) of South Africa. The intention was to probe the imprint of exile, the military wing uMkhonto weSizwe (MK, 'The Spear of the Nation'), prison, underground organisation, the United Democratic Front (UDF) and a variety of other influences, in order to gauge the salience of these different experiences – many of them arising from people's own belief systems predating membership of any organisation – for the current character and potential trajectory of the ANC.

As the title of this book suggests, the project has narrowed down to one feature: the underground operation. But the earlier scope has not been lost entirely. Indeed, the definition of underground organisation that is adopted here is a wide one, incorporating several of the original themes. This is because there are many interfaces, overlaps and intersections in practice. Instead of seeing exile and 'internal' underground activities, or prison and underground, as distinct experiences, we need to be alive to their connections and interrelationship.

The ANC leadership came to be located outside the country from the mid- to late 1960s. Exile was in many ways intimately connected with underground organisation, for it was in exile that many people were trained or briefed to perform the acts they undertook as operatives inside South Africa. It was often in exile that operations were planned, though the degree of autonomy allowed 'inside' would vary. It was from exile that many underground groups were supplied, and from where various forms of logistical and financial support were provided. It was also in the interaction between the inside and outside that intelligence was gathered and evaluated on many important issues. Since elements of the exile experience clearly underpinned underground organisation and activity – its operation, success or failure – I treat them as an integral part of the subject.[1] To do otherwise could lead to an artificial focus on either exile or the underground as the single dynamising force; for example, it is often believed, especially by those who spent their struggle period in exile, that the establishment of underground units required exile initiation first. It also tends to see 'being ANC' as purely those who were formally inducted and provided with membership cards. This, it will be argued, excludes the large numbers who associated themselves as 'freelance' ANC activists, not being able to link up with formal structures or not trying to for security reasons.

Prison experience also fed directly into one phase of the development of the underground, especially in the early 1970s, just as it later helped the achievement of 'Congress hegemony' in the legal space that opened in the late 1970s. In some cases, prisoners were specifically mandated to join a particular underground unit on leaving prison. It was within prison too that many former Black Consciousness-aligned members 'converted' to the ANC-led liberation movement, and they were among those deployed to underground activities or specific units. Many of the prisoners who came back from Robben Island were able to give leadership, guidance and advice on organising, either because they had been leaders before imprisonment or because the hothouse atmosphere of the Island was a place of training. Thus they emerged able to transmit their skills to others, first in underground organisation and later when the public space for democratic organisation opened up.

One of the reasons for focusing primarily on underground organisation is that, precisely because of its secret character, much of what was undertaken and achieved might otherwise never appear in the historical record. The often anonymous practitioners are passing away year by year. Some documentary evidence exists of those who were arrested and tried in court but the same is not true of the many operatives who were never captured and remain unknown. There is thus some urgency to capture the story before the actors disappear. While this is true for all sites of the struggle it is most acute for the underground, because of its high degree of secrecy. In many cases we do not know who we are looking for, because very few participants were allowed to know what they were engaging in – at the time most people did not even realise that there was such work afoot.

While underground work has a connection with other forms of struggle, it has specific ways and places of functioning that distinguish it from them. It also raises complex moral, social and psychological issues that do not arise in the same way in other spheres of action. There is something extreme and often hermetic in the demands on the life of the underground operative which is not found in other forms of struggle. The people concerned made harsh choices that often led them to pay a heavy price in their personal life and opportunities for personal fulfilment. The struggle made demands that ensured that what is called 'normal life' was seldom possible. At the same time the moral issues that arose, and opportunities that the same secret life provided for both noble deeds and abuse, are worth exploring; and we shall also look at some of its effects that still keep people from functioning adequately in the present-day environment. We are dealing with a category of people many of whom may be experiencing, knowingly or not, the effects of post-traumatic stress in a fairly extreme form.

Some of what emerged in the course of this study was not anticipated. In particular, the ideological beliefs and obligations associated with membership of the ANC and the South African Communist Party (SACP) were reinforced by ideas, practices and obligations of other belief systems, especially those that may for convenience be described as 'traditional'. We touch on this intersection below in Chapter 6,[2] and also relate it to the notion that a national liberation struggle involves individuals with a range of distinct identities, some of which have not been adequately recognised in ANC thinking. While these issues have received considerable attention in Zimbabwean historiography, they have been relatively neglected in writings on the struggle in South Africa.[3]

Another issue whose significance was not initially anticipated is that of gender. In this work there is an attempt to uncover the overall gendered character of the ANC as manifested in underground organisation, gendered notions of the personal, heroism, and masculinities and femininities, as well as the potential and actual experience of abuse as it arose within underground activity. The discourse of many ANC leaders was suffused with masculinist idioms; this is contextualised and explained. The intersection of belief systems was also of gender significance within the ANC, not least where the practice of initiation was connected to underground recruitment; the transition to manhood entailed ideas that need to be seen and discussed in the context of struggle.

The whole topic of gender arises more broadly in the general character of underground struggle, and possibly in a whole range of other revolutionary pursuits that tend to be treated as heroic (and, in some literature, as therefore performed by men). It is evident in the way that women were involved and deployed in MK and the underground generally. The evidence that follows points to a complexity and conditionality that much feminist literature does not adequately acknowledge. We touch on the notion of heroism and the manifold gender relations it may embody.

Revolutionary work impacts on the individual as an autonomous person. This study examines the fit between the organisation and the personal in matters of individual judgement, and also how interpersonal relations and conceptions of love tended to be displaced by revolutionary notions of 'love for the people' and the 'ANC as family'.

This book does not purport to be an exhaustive account of the history of the ANC-led underground, though it uncovers aspects of that history that have not been previously researched or recorded. It is a rereading of the early ANC and SACP underground and the conditions of the time in the light of existing documentation and new oral evidence. It was expected that the oral evidence would throw up new materials and insights; some of the received written history of struggle is also now shown to be open to reinterpretation, with potentially important modifications that perhaps introduce new ways of understanding.

In particular this study challenges the prevailing historiography of the underground, which speaks of the absence of the ANC–SACP in the period between the Rivonia Trial and 1976.[4] While we must concede their invisibility, which was a condition for their survival, we shall see that activity involving the ANC and SACP continued after 1964 at varying levels of intensity.[5]

The study also suggests the possibility of a greater underground presence than even the ANC documentation has claimed. This is because the ANC relied primarily on reports from officially constituted units, while this study takes cognisance of the wide range of freelance, de facto ANC underground activities that were mounted. The new information comes from oral evidence; this book draws far more on oral sources than most previous accounts, and still the record is by no means complete. A full account would require many years of further work. Research is still needed in many areas of South Africa where important events took place, but this requires extensive funding, much time for travel and interviews, and linguistic resources that are not presently available to this researcher.[6] We need to recognise that without a wider geographical reach our history will remain heavily urban-biased. The South African Democratic Education Trust (SADET) has taken important steps towards remedying the problem, but would no doubt acknowledge the considerable scope that remains.

Saying that a historical account is geographically limited is not just a matter of 'finishing a job', but may change meanings, for practices in the neglected areas may vary substantially from those in the big cities and, if recorded, lead to substantially new interpretations. Some cases that bring quite different, new evidence to the fore appear in later chapters.

◎

This book refers to actions by individuals or organisations that are meant to be outside the public eye, though they may be designed for a public impact. In other cases the activity could be covert because mere survival, albeit out of sight, may demand an underground existence of which the public has no knowledge.

Underground political activity or organisation covers a wide range of situations, some of which may be perfectly legal. Subterfuge could be used to achieve political objectives in conditions where openness would make this difficult or impossible. It could also protect people perceived as being at risk in the struggle against the state. Legality, where it existed, was always fragile, and some of what was legal had to be done without official knowledge and in secrecy.

Underground work is political activity that is not open or openly declared for what it is. Under cover of doing one thing, a person may be performing another invisibly. In clandestine action, whatever does or does not happen on the surface, the politically significant activity is done unseen. Sometimes underground and 'above ground' coexist for purely practical purposes, as when an above-ground person faces the chance of being detained by the police after someone else's arrest. The person at risk may have to 'disappear' or have a low profile or stay at some secret place until it is clear whether or not the danger is real.

In some situations where people have rights or apparent freedom of political activity, they may nevertheless be under surveillance or be treated as if they had no legal right to exist; and it may be vital that what they are doing (or part of it) is not observed by the police. Sometimes the activity may be illegal but the organisation may not have been banned, as was the case in the 1980s when the UDF and its affiliated organisations were generally still legal but the State of Emergency prohibited certain activities, especially in areas like the Northern Transvaal (see Chapter 5). Continuing these activities underground was not generally seen as implying a permanent illegal underground existence.

People in full hiding do not surface at all. Everything about them is invisible. They might have a distinct appearance known only to a few or to those who do not know whom they are dealing with. Alternatively one may have a public face, quite distinct from the underground one, that will not be seen publicly and will only appear in disguised form or to a restricted range of people.

Illegal underground activity has often coexisted with completely legal activities, though the style of activity changed substantially at various times. This was the case when the Communist Party was reconstituted as an illegal organisation but its members still participated quite legally in the Congress Alliance (see Chapter 3 below). Likewise, in the 1970s and 1980s some activists participated in legal organisations, including UDF affiliates, while they were engaged in illegal underground activity for the ANC and SACP. Whether such combinations of legal and illegal were possible, and when and how they were achieved, would depend on the strength of the forces of repression and how well this was matched by the liberation movement.

We have already touched on a point that became more of a factor with the establishment of the ANC in exile: What are the boundaries of underground activities? This relates to both place and time. The present work does not classify an activity as underground purely according to when and where it was finally executed. The preparatory phases are part of the exercise, even if they happened much earlier and in another country. In fact, preparatory phases for entering South Africa often involved great danger and setting up a wide range of logistical arrangements or the acquisition of very specific skills. Success or failure often related to the level of training.

◎

Little has been written on underground activity in South Africa. The reasons are fairly obvious: much of it was illegal and suggests by its very clandestine nature that the practitioner did not wish to be identified. Most published material is confined to pages or chapters of biographies or autobiographies, and these are primarily of leaders. There is a wealth of archival material but, besides offering only partial evidence (as in court records) or being difficult to access (as in the actual reports of ANC operatives), they cannot provide the wide focus and full texture which this study seeks and which oral evidence is better able to give.

Given the limitations of the existing literature, I decided to concentrate primarily on oral testimony by conducting interviews with former underground operatives. Because this is not purely a historical study, it was important that the evidence gathered should not be constrained by being presented or recorded for very distinct purposes, as is the case with the courtroom record and many other archival documents. These are generally unconcerned with extracting the social character and meanings of how people were organised and what was done. Court cases are especially problematic in that a whole range of evidence that led to the decision to commit what would become a 'criminal act' does not form part of the 'facts in issue', as the legal phrase has it. The meaning of the political activity becomes known in a very truncated form, and the primary body of testimony of the accused may well remain in lawyer's notes or go unrecorded in any way, as not admissible in the court.

The arguments for oral evidence are compelling. Many informants are old and will die without their story being told if it is not recorded now. At present, there is no longer any surviving member of the Communist Party of South Africa Central Committee of 1950, which decided to dissolve the Party. Many people may already have died without it being known that they had engaged in underground activities. There is also the fact that underground personnel are mostly unknown people. Interviewing them brings them and their actions into the public domain, as they deserve. Such sources sometimes also reveal that certain people who were known as collaborators with the apartheid regime in fact also assisted ANC–SACP or MK units. Instead of dying despised as traitors, they should be acknowledged for their involvement in the struggle, under the most difficult of conditions; their role certainly adds complexity to the historiography and sociology of the struggle. Lastly, as with all oral material, the researcher has the opportunity to probe for further information in the interviews. This option is obviously unavailable with archival material.

There are well-documented dangers in conducting oral work. Some informants may not want to 'tell all', out of loyalty to the ANC or because of covert habits of operation which remain with many people long after they have stopped working in those conditions. There is also the difficulty of verifying information especially where there are few survivors. Respondents sometimes tend to inflate their role and even to invent an underground *persona* or part. All these points must be taken into account. Luckily, in the evidence presented in this work, there are only a few cases which appear to be uncorroborated or hard to believe. I have indicated where some claims may be exaggerated, but in general they seem credible and likely to stand the test of scrutiny. The claims made in this study are well within reasonable belief; they were made in interviews between 2000 and 2005, as listed on pages 168–70. Not all the speakers were activists; and tentative information is stated as such.

I interviewed 54 people for this book. Nine were women; two informants were former Security Police, one of whom wished to be anonymous. Readers may be interested in the distribution of the sample between those in exile and those who were internally based, but this is hard to classify. Many went out for training and returned to perform operations; others never left the country but spent much of their time in prison. The majority of those interviewed were Africans, only four being white, five Indian and two Coloured. The age groups and periods and places of origin and activity of the informants varied considerably. Informants on much of the struggle time were both veterans and relatively young people who had come from the Black Consciousness movement. This younger group has provided evidence that underlines the generally unacknowledged degree of overlap between ANC and Black Consciousness. While most interviews took place in major cities like Cape Town, Johannesburg, Pretoria, Durban and Pietermaritzburg, others were held in a range of smaller places including those in rural Transkei, Limpopo and North-West Province; and some of the informants came from those places.

I made special efforts to record the experiences of rank-and-file underground workers. Some of the leadership sources were very articulate but had not taken part in the actual building of structures. Leaders were good sources where they knew the theory well and provided good manuscript material; those at the grassroots were sometimes much less clear and systematic in presenting their recollections – but they knew more about the dangers, problems and other practical matters.

I came to place greater weight on the small but vital contribution of those who may often have been designated as minor players but whose role was nevertheless vital in the execution of underground activity. One of the veterans, Joe Matthews, has objected that this bias tends to underrate the impact of giants like Moses Kotane.[7] The balance is difficult, but what is clear is that, while Kotane is known and much of his work is documented, many who feature in the following pages have not been part of the historical literature, even though they have made history. Often the status of underground combatant was incorrectly restricted to people physically engaged in military acts, yet others who undertook vital preparatory work were also exposed to great danger. Many such individuals and the type of activities they engaged in were previously unknown to me.

◎

In addition to discussing the pitfalls of collecting oral testimony, I must locate myself as author, indicating what influences I may have brought to bear on the interviews and the study in general – location, it has been said, is as important in scholarship as it is in real estate.[8] As a former figure in the liberation movement with a leadership role, my own *persona* could have affected the answers I got. The incorrect perception that the interviewer still occupies a position of power in the organisation may lead informants, if they think they fall lower in the hierarchy, to supply answers to please the interviewer or which they believe may enhance their status within the organisation. This is part of wider ANC notions of hierarchies and seniority that persist even after their formal status may have ended. It is especially the case with those who have been in military structures.[9] Most of the respondents were, however, people unlikely to have such motives in mind and in many cases were very well established or semi-retired and were not overawed by me and in no need of my intervention for securing jobs or anything else.

In so far as many of the interviews were with women, certain experiences that they may have undergone would be revealed more readily to a female. I am aware that I may not have heard the whole of every story, for one or other reason; and that women may have felt constraints about relating certain incidents to a man.

Another factor was that I, an English-speaking white South African, was interviewing mainly Africans in their second language. All interviews were conducted in English. I believe that this was not much of an obstacle for my informants, most of whom were very proficient in English; several held leadership positions. The bulk of the key policy documents were almost exclusively in English.

That I am a white South African may have influenced the type of responses that I received at times, but almost all the informants were used to engaging with whites on political matters. Also, a measure of trust existed because of my political history, which may have made my whiteness a less significant factor. At this point, let me sketch my own background.

I grew up as a middle-class white and considered myself a liberal for much of my early life. In 1968 I held my first academic position at the University of Cape Town, where I corresponded with Professor Jack Simons (banned at the time, and living in Zambia), the legendary Marxist theorist and my former lecturer, but our relationship had little political content and related almost purely to customary law. As a liberal I gradually came to feel that I had reached a dead end politically, and when I was awarded a scholarship to study overseas at the end of 1969 I intended to find a way to return and participate in illegal activities. That gradually crystallised from vague ideas into recruitment by the SACP to work underground in Durban, mainly issuing pamphlets through the conventional post. As preparation I received some political training from Rusty Bernstein in a rather orthodox form of Marxism that seemed to be out of touch with what I had been reading in journals like *New Left Review* and *Monthly Review*. I received technical training from Ronnie Kasrils. My formal recruitment and briefing on my overall operations in the four years from 1971 until 1975, before my first arrest, took place under the oversight of Joe Slovo.

Although technically part of the ANC's military wing, MK, my training was fairly rudimentary; it was in surveillance and countersurveillance, modes of secret communication, and a brief introduction to using explosives. The main thrust was equipping me with a variety of methods of propaganda distribution. Because of the dangers of the time and the fear of suffering losses when so few people of this type were in the field, there was great reluctance to have me work with others.

I was offered a temporary and later a permanent lecturing position at the University of Natal in Durban, first in African studies, then in law. Time was needed to settle into the illegal work. It was necessary to establish that I was beyond any suspicion. I also needed time to find the equipment and suitable places for the work. In fact, suitable conditions were never found; the resources at my disposal led me to run most of my activities from my home. I had been given 200 British pounds and, although I was content with that sum, I could not entertain elaborate plans or operations.

Over the four years of my work I disseminated formal publications of the SACP and, to some extent, the ANC. During my visit to London in 1974, after the Portuguese coup, a more optimistic mood led Kasrils and Slovo to be better disposed to recruiting others (a hasty decision that was to prove unwise) and to my producing a publication myself. The text was designed to enable the ANC to react immediately to events with a clear sense of what was happening in the country at the time. It was called *Vukani! / Awake!*

On various occasions I was asked to perform other tasks whose import I did not grasp at the time. I had some years added to my later prison sentence because I readdressed a letter to a particular person who, it later turned out, was in a group of guerrillas captured after landing on the coast of Natal. Under interrogation and torture I admitted to readdressing this letter. At another stage I was asked to gather information about the occupants of a particular house. It turned out that there was no house with the address that was supplied.

I was arrested in June 1975 and then spent a total of eight years in prison, a period that, because of the discussions with my fellow inmates, enriched my political understanding a great deal. The practice at that point had been for many released prisoners to leave South Africa instead of being confined under house arrest and having their political activities constrained. As we saw the situation in the country change in the early years of PW Botha's leadership, the collective inside the prison decided that I should remain within South Africa.[10]

Although I was party to this decision and agreed with it, it was not without a degree of dread that I anticipated returning to circumstances that might (and did in fact) lead to my re-arrest. I kept a fairly low profile at first, but gradually, after preparing the TB Davie Memorial lecture on the Freedom Charter,[11] I found myself drawn more intensely into the activities of the UDF.

The period from my release until the unbanning of the ANC and SACP in 1990 was one in which many people like me participated in legal activities but were in varying ways connected to the underground. From the beginning I participated in legal activities but also met separately with others sometimes in a small group, sometimes one-on-one. This implicit trust never led to my being part of a formally constituted underground unit, partly because my background might have jeopardised the existence of such a group. But I interacted with likeminded people as a formal unit might have done.

Also, throughout this period I received 'emissaries' from leaders outside the country, sometimes asking me to do one thing or another, such as starting a theoretical journal, or telling people who approached me, to work with me. When a person was 'instructed' to link up with me or with someone else in a similar situation, it was often also an instruction to break off links with a particular faction. The 1980s was a period manifesting serious factional divisions within the country, mainly related to control of resources but also sometimes reflecting sharp ideological divisions.

In the middle of this time, during the State of Emergency of 1985/6, I was forced to go underground to avoid arrest for a period of about nine months, using some of the techniques I had learnt from Kasrils but had never had to employ in the 1970s. I re-emerged with the lifting of the State of Emergency but from time to time it was normal for people in my position to disappear temporarily whenever there was the possibility of arrest. I was, however, redetained in the 1986 State of Emergency, kept for 27 months and released into stringent house-arrest conditions in September 1988.[12] One year later I defied these to attend the adoption of the Harare Declaration in Zimbabwe and remained out of the country for five months.

Returning to South Africa at the end of January 1990 I did not know what fate awaited me but acted as if I was a free person. Fortunately, a few days later the ANC and SACP were unbanned and the restrictions I was supposed to be under were lifted. I was drawn into ANC and SACP leadership in the period 1990–1. In the course of meetings I saw something of the inner workings of the two organisations, which also bears on what appears in this book, for example ANC attempts to veto Chris Hani's leaving full-time employment in the organisation to work full-time for the SACP.

In the 1980s I attempted to depict myself as pursuing a purely legal course, which carried little weight with the Security Police. More significantly for this study, it was not the perception of those activists who themselves wanted to engage in illegal activities. This meant that I was repeatedly approached to advise as to how or whether someone should join MK. While I was careful not to be trapped in police set-ups, this was part of my life. Also, from the very early days of my first release from prison, I was drawn into situations where young Africans, in particular, asked me to take them through various banned texts. This had not been how I envisaged 're-establishing' myself as an apparently law-abiding citizen.

More dramatically, on my release from detention and house arrest in 1988 I was one day taken to meet someone who turned out to be Mac Maharaj, then leading the Vula operation.[13] It was difficult to operate actively in Vula while under the type of surveillance entailed in house arrest. But the procession of people approaching me to get involved in illegal activities continued, and in one case I was able to steer towards Vula a person who was able to offer access to and use of an entire factory.

In brief, then, the experiences that I have undergone have given me some practical insights into the types of problems, conflicts and other issues that arise in an underground situation. This background is a substantial factor informing the way I read literature and interpret interview material. It has affected the questions I ask and how I have probed the information provided. It has also affected whom I have relied on as informants, in some cases substantially different from other scholars. This is because what I know about some people from the struggle has provided me with information not in the possession of conventional researchers. It is sometimes assumed that a scholarly background is rendered suspect where the researcher has also been an active participant in the activities about which he or she writes. One colleague has suggested that my work comes under far greater scrutiny than that of people who have been less involved or 'kept their distance'. I am quite happy for this work to be subjected to the closest scrutiny. At the same time it is necessary to address the question of partisanship or 'positionality'. There is a difference between partisanship (in the sense of believing in democracy, supporting national liberation and transformation) and a willingness to draw conclusions that are not sustained by evidence or presenting evidence that is false or otherwise flawed. These are basic scholarly canons all researchers are supposed to abide by whether or not they have been politically committed or involved in advancing a cause.

At the same time, I contest the idea that political involvement may be a *disability* that needs to be overcome in order to engage in serious scholarship. In fact, it is precisely because I have been an underground operative that it is possible for me to ask questions that do not easily present themselves to someone who knows little about such activity. That kind of innocence or inexperience makes it difficult to assess what constitutes an adequate underground operation or what is entailed in 'professional' or less well-prepared and -executed operations. As indicated earlier, this may influence one's assessment of the credibility of sources.

'Rules' of underground organisation exist that need to be observed, and if the informant does not refer to them, the interviewer needs to know what to ask in order to establish whether or not these were observed, and the degree of care that was taken to protect secrecy or to ensure the successful execution of the work. Were all individuals adequately protected against danger? Even if an act was successfully performed, were risks taken that could have compromised the operation or the security of individuals? Underground operatives tend to take some things for granted that have not been documented, about how they communicate, what they do and do not do, how they advance and retreat, what the range of options may be, how they collect weapons or dispose of literature. Many variations arise, but it is precisely in knowing what to ask in relation to these questions and choices that my having been an operative is an advantage. Knowing the 'tools of the trade' provides a basis for assessing how adequately the underground tasks were performed.

While arguing that my background has not been a scholarly disqualification or disadvantage, I do not deny that 'outsiders,' by virtue of having been uninvolved, may see things that are not observed by 'insiders' who are or were very closely connected to the question being studied. They may also conduct interviews which yield similar material to mine, though there is an element of suspicion that they would have to overcome, given the wariness of operatives, especially towards those unconnected with the struggle.

The conditions of struggle demanded tight discipline and 'holding the line' – securing the hegemony of the positions held by the liberation movement – under very hostile conditions. It was dangerous to do this, and dealing with the danger was often incompatible with debate over complexities that may have related to the issues which were being advanced and which provided a more complex understanding. This, and constraints on their time, tended to close cadres off from currents of thinking that many scholars could access; what these scholars read and wrote about may throw fresh light on the overall liberation and underground experience. Stepping back from active involvement, I too have found that I see certain questions differently. Some of the questions raised in the chapters that follow are ones I had not asked when I was actively engaged.

◎

This book is at once an attempt to document and explain a *phase* and also a *species* of struggle against apartheid covered by the ANC–SACP alliance. Underground activity occurred mainly during the period of illegality after the banning of the SACP and ANC, though, as will be seen, there were elements of underground organisation earlier on.

This study cannot be seen, therefore, purely as a work of history, though it is presented as a contribution towards rescuing and preserving what has gone unrecorded and bringing some of the invisible to light. It also seeks to explain elements of the past that have previously gone unnoticed or been totally unknown to the public, or about which there has been silence or where the interpretation of their significance needs, in my view, to be reconsidered.

The chapters that follow also interrogate this history as a pattern of social and political activity that has affected interpersonal relations and modes of conduct in society, including gender relations. The character of the problem under consideration, a species of human activity, can only be understood in all its complexity if one does not set limits on the range of disciplines which one uses. In trying to understand these, I have drawn on insights from a number of disciplines, in particular history, political science, sociology, gender studies and social anthropology. Likewise, another problem could well be easily disposed of through a much narrower range of paradigms and disciplinary sources. This study is best described as both a history and a broadly sociological and gendered analysis of underground organisation as a political phenomenon.

The underground was generally meant to be invisible except when an act was performed. The actors were meant to be unknown. Sometimes they had to be silent about their work, though that was intended to be temporary. This book tries to probe silences in another sense, that is not necessarily consciously suppressed information, activities and understandings, but what many participants may not themselves have understood or had time to consider about their own activities. In a context of danger and the prospect of death and torture, few had the time to reflect on the multiple meanings of the work they conducted and what it meant in terms of their own subjective choices as individuals. These were choices made when there was no idea of reward and the most likely prospect was arrest and death or torture. The liberation movement generally did not see people as total beings but as individuals suited for particular activities. This book considers the conditions outside the direct organisational and operational work, and looks at how people saw their own identity and their interrelationship with others who were their equal or more powerful, and tries to reflect these more fully than in previous work on this historical narrative.

Throughout, the individual becomes a key informant. Most of what is known to scholars is in the already written word, albeit open to reinterpretation. The individuals in the pages that follow often add what might otherwise have remained unknown, and never have been recorded. They also see and interpret events from their unique perspectives, just as (whether they acknowledge it or not) scholars bring their own 'baggage' in interpreting data. Probing the individual accounts often raises issues that may not have been mentioned in earlier phases of the research process; or what may have been seen initially as subsidiary in interview gains a new importance, so that it increases in value in future explanations and interpretations.

Informants are bearers of heritage. Already there has been some communication of this heritage, as in the well-known life and example of Albertina Sisulu. In cities and villages throughout the land, these heritage-bearers became a force through which new cadres were built, educated in the history of the struggle, learning how the ANC and its allies pursued liberation in ways that were in certain respects distinct from that of other political movements.

One feature that emerges when considering what was discussed and not written down at the time is that we need to rethink the standard way that ANC history has tended to be periodised by dates, often as rough decades with certain dominant features. The 1950s, for instance, has been viewed as a time of legal nonviolent struggle; yet there was murmuring about armed struggle at the time, and uniforms and oaths adopted by the Congress volunteers all signalled the discipline required for military activity. This is just one example of the blurring of distinctions between periods and phases of struggle that deserves revisiting. Similarly, it is the foundations started by the Revd (later Canon) James Calata and Dr AB Xuma back in the 1940s for the building of the ANC as an organised force, that help to contextualise the achievements of the Youth League and the 1950s as a continuation of earlier efforts. The illegality of the ANC and underground coexisted with some individuals continuing to work as if they were still within a constitutionally recognised organisation. There were ruptures in continuities and continuities within ruptures, which means that history needs to be seen in a more fluid way without rigid separations between phases.

2

THE EARLY UNDERGROUND

From the M-Plan to Rivonia

In 1953 the ANC agreed in secret at its annual conference that a plan be drawn up to enable the movement to operate underground in the likely event that it would be banned by the Nationalist government. This became known as the M-Plan or the Mandela Plan. Most historians of the period have downplayed the M-Plan, seeing it as having had little influence on the ANC, especially after the organisation was banned in 1960. They have also written off the early phase of illegal underground activity after 1960 as amateurish, evidence of a lack of preparation and foresight on the ANC's part and of its having been caught off guard by what was depicted and widely perceived as an all-powerful white state.

The evidence, however, suggests a more complicated picture, requiring considerable qualification. In fact the M-Plan had far wider impact than has been recognised. Indeed, it formed the basis for establishing the ANC underground immediately after banning and reappeared as a basis for organisation in later phases of the struggle right into the 1980s, in both rural and urban areas. What is more, the early years of preparation for underground work form an important strand of ANC history, starting with the adoption of the M-Plan in 1953 and a range of other activities, as this chapter will show. Many of the traits associated with the ANC are usually attributed to the exile experience but can also be traced to this formative period of the 1950s. The M-Plan therefore deserves to be revisited. The traits are real features of the ANC, but this is not to say that its members behaved in a fixed, unvarying way. In fact the notion of ANC culture is wider than the organisation, in that it is embedded within families and other social organisms that sustain the ANC and its practices.

Some activists envisaged the possibility of illegal action long before it became necessary. Ray Alexander Simons, when preparing to emigrate to South Africa in 1929, was trained by Latvian Communists for underground work.[1] They believed that even though the Communist Party of South Africa, as it was then called, was a legal organisation, people had to prepare for the possibility of illegality. In addition, about fourteen South African Communists were educated in Comintern (Communist International) schools or universities, which ran a compulsory course on underground organisation.[2] Among those trained in this way were leading ANC and SACP figures like Moses Kotane, JB Marks and the Communist trade unionist Bettie du Toit.[3] Comintern representatives also visited South Africa and interacted with South African Communists, while South African Communists visited the Comintern to consult, attend meetings or study. These activities were largely secret, underground operations.[4] Despite periodic urging by the Comintern, the training they received was not supplemented by plans for an underground.

It has been claimed that the ideas embraced in the M-Plan were first advanced by the Africanist thinker and then leading ANC Youth League figure A P Mda, who apparently called for development of a cell system and preparation for underground. These plans were forwarded to Nelson Mandela at the time of the ANC national conference in December 1951 but were considered too dangerous.[5] According to some members of the PAC, the 'M' in the M-Plan referred to Mda and not Mandela.[6] Though Mda may well have had these ideas first, it was in their later form associated with Nelson Mandela that they achieved the organisational significance considered here.

The M-Plan was prompted by the belief that political conditions were changing towards much greater repression. There were clear signs in, for example, the banning of the Communist Party in 1950 and the restriction of many leading figures in the Congress movement.[7] Some members felt it necessary for the ANC to organise itself in a way that adapted to these new conditions, as it was no longer possible to assume that ANC objectives could be achieved through public activity such as huge rallies and very large branches. Since it was likely that there would be a clampdown and that the ANC would be banned, there had to be a greater sensitivity about security. The ANC had to begin to work in smaller units and with greater secrecy.[8] In January 1953 Joe Matthews, then a young ANC leader, wrote to his father, Professor ZK Matthews, Cape leader of the ANC, about 'a secret meeting ... of the top leaders of both the SAIC [South African Indian Congress] & ANC, half of whom were banned', at which they had planned the future with 'cold-blooded realism'. 'Broadly speaking the idea is to strengthen the organisation tremendously. To prepare for the continuation of the organisation under conditions of illegality by organising on the basis of the cell system. The continuation of the [Defiance] Campaign and its widening into the mass campaign and Industrial Action.'[9]

Matthews recalled that meeting, over fifty years later, saying that 'there were very strong feelings that sooner or later the organisation would be banned and that certain preparations should be made.' But the repression or the expected scale of it did not follow immediately:

It took seven years before the bannings actually took place. But I think the reason people felt that bannings were imminent arose from the steps which the government was taking against the organisation, against meetings of more than 10 people that were banned in various areas. It turned out that that was temporary ...

But as a matter of fact, gradually after the Defiance Campaign, things returned to what one might call 'South African normality'. Meetings began again, conferences were held again, the national conference of the ANC in Queenstown was held in 1953 ... Life in fact went on. The Congress of Democrats was formed in 1953, meetings of the joint executives were held. The campaign for the Congress of the People proceeded. So the declaration of banning of ANC occurred much later but they had sort of prepared for it.[10]

Preparation of the M-Plan was initially approved in secret at the 1953 ANC conference, which Nelson Mandela was prevented from attending (being banned).[11] Mandela confirms that it seemed inevitable that the state would 'attempt to put us out of business as a legal organization as soon as it could.'[12] It was on the basis of that reasoning, shared by many others, that he motivated for and was mandated to develop a contingency plan for the organisation to operate underground.[13]

While the decision may initially have been taken in secret, it did not remain so, and over the years that followed it was publicly known and debated.

The M-Plan embraced a number of features. It may have been conceived simply as a preparation for the potential future underground existence of the ANC as a whole. It may have also had a more limited purpose, namely greater security, to prevent the ANC from falling victim to the mounting repression.[14] But it was also an extension of modes of operation that had already been adopted and followed. Many of the leaders, despite being subjected to heavy banning orders, continued carrying out Congress activities in secret, meeting among themselves and with those of their colleagues who were still allowed to operate legally.[15] According to Walter Sisulu, the M-Plan was 'actually intended to go into effect when banning orders began to take place'.[16] About Sisulu's activities, the Security Police noted at the time:

> After Sisulu was restricted, his public activities decreased to such an extent that he no longer came into the limelight … However, he has dug himself in (established his position) and there is plenty of evidence from utterly reliable and delicate sources that he is, in secret and behind the scenes, as busy as before with advice and guidance and instigation among the non-whites.[17]

After Sisulu's banning, Oliver Tambo was made Secretary-General of the ANC in 1955, but because of his work as a lawyer he could not manage the full-time organisational work. Sisulu therefore continued to work in a full-time capacity underground, with Tambo empowered to veto whatever he did. In effect, Sisulu remained de facto Secretary-General.[18]

The M-Plan did not follow the classic concept of a tightly knit vanguard-type underground. Despite the tighter security involved, it also envisaged expanding the membership and organisation.[19] While the Communist Party underground was modelled on Leninist vanguard lines, albeit operating in a situation where much Communist effort went into building the ANC, the ANC underground was conceived as a way of enabling a mass movement to operate in illegal conditions.[20]

In this sense, the M-Plan can be seen as a moment of transition and also of rupture within the ANC opposition politics of the time.[21] Already, some leaders identified the Defiance Campaign as marking a break with the past, even a revolutionary break. In the words of Walter Sisulu:

> It had the effect of making the people confident and fearless, prepared to defy the laws, to be prepared to go to jail and meet any situation. That was the importance of it. It was the beginning of a new situation, which led even to a person facing the death penalty with confidence. The Campaign brought about a situation in which people were not arrested just by chance, but by plan. This meant organisation ... The movement called for volunteers. In the Eastern Cape, it was called 'Amadela Kufa', 'defiers of death'. You can see from this that a revolutionary situation was emerging.[22]

If these tendencies have been correctly identified, then the break between the mass activity of the 1950s and underground and revolutionary politics started earlier than 1960, however uneven the character of this rupture may have been. (It manifested in other ways too, which will be indicated in the course of the narrative.) That was certainly the understanding of Sisulu, who was possibly the key organisational figure, first as Secretary-General and later as *de facto* Secretary-General underground. Sisulu depicted the M-Plan as part of a transition towards greater militancy. As with the armed struggle, underground organisation was not just forced on the ANC as a 'last resort', but had been in preparation long before illegality and the formation of MK. Many people, including Sisulu and Mandela themselves, were talking about armed activity in the early 1950s, long before the official decision was taken by the ANC.

Preliminary preparations for armed struggle, we now know, can be detected in the arrangement made between Mandela and Sisulu that Sisulu should seek support for such activity while visiting China in the early 1950s. They can also be seen in the almost simultaneous discussions in Sekhukhuneland, influenced very much by the Mau Mau struggle, and similar sentiments to 'fight back' in other parts of South Africa.[23] Likewise, the first plans for underground, in the M-Plan, were elaborated some seven years before banning (and almost at the same time as the underground reconstitution of the SACP). In fact the 1950s was not simply a period of mass militancy but also, in the thinking of many, of preparation for the likelihood of illegal and military struggle.

The use of a volunteer corps wearing uniforms and swearing an oath during the Defiance Campaign also points towards the type of discipline that would be required for military organisation. Clothing is a form of communication whose meanings may be ambiguous: 'It is ... a social artifact – a form of communication. ... Clothing ... [is] a system of signs that derives meaning from its context while enabling us to carry on our activities. In turn, changes in clothing serve as a means of accommodating and facilitating changes in their context.'[24] A uniform may mean one or more thing depending on the type of clothing, the context and other surrounding factors. Changed clothing may signify that there are wider changes afoot. The Congress Volunteers uniform may have been interpreted in more than one way by those who swore the oath; such a uniform had a potential for military connotations, as happened when the Indian nationalist Subhas Chandra Bose introduced military drills and uniforms for a volunteer corps at a time when the Congress of India was committed to peaceful struggle. He later went on to form the Indian National Army.[25]

A uniform implies individuals united for a single purpose, and together with an oath where one commits oneself to follow instructions it may be one of the prerequisites for the type of discipline required in future military action. The oath signed by volunteers read:

I, the undersigned, Volunteer of the National Volunteer Corps, do hereby solemnly pledge and bind myself to serve my country and my people in accordance with the directive of the National Volunteer Corps and to participate fully and without reservations to the best of my ability in the Campaign for the Defiance of Unjust Laws. I shall obey the orders of my leader under whom I shall be placed and strictly abide by the rules and regulations of the National Volunteer Corps framed from time to time. It shall be my duty to keep myself physically, mentally and morally fit.[26]

As far as I am aware, such a submission to organisational authority was unprecedented in ANC history. It indicated the birth of something new, beyond a distinct set of clothes. It suggested an unconditional commitment to defiance and to abiding by the authority of leadership, implicitly delegitimating the authority of the day. Taken together, these factors indicate that the current division of the history of the ANC into rigid periods characterised by specific activities, for example the 'announcement' of the formation of MK in 1961, needs revisiting; as we have seen, life is really more fluid, and the 'type' of organisation in any decade can often overlap with that of another decade where it is 'not supposed to happen'. Recognising the problems with these rigid distinctions between periods will help us understand better how ideas brew in people's minds for some time, or are manifested before they exist formally, or continue in practice after their 'time has passed' – so that they are sometimes dangerous or a problem organisationally in other ways .

As with all plans for underground operations, the M-Plan envisaged a hierarchy with a clear 'top-down' character. In Mandela's words, 'The idea was to set up organisational machinery that would allow the ANC to take decisions at the highest level, which could then be swiftly transmitted to the organisation as a whole without calling a meeting.'[27] The same emphasis can be found in the description of how the M-Plan was implemented in East London, given by Johnson Malcomess Mgabela:

> Going from house to house we spoke with the people *and gave them some orders*, trying to bring political understanding of what the ANC were doing. We had to organise small meetings because the government declared any meeting of more than ten people an illegal gathering. So we used the Mandela Plan: going to a house; staying there with ten people; giving them an understanding of what the ANC was doing; *giving them orders*; going to the next house. We tried to give people a message of what the ANC stood for and what its plans of actions were. You would tell people here, tell people there. You would even go to a public place like a shebeen or stand with a few people on a street corner. After a few days you would find that you had told a few hundred people about the policies and activities of the ANC. All of this was to be done underground. No name must be written down. Everything must be kept in secret. From the national level the *instructions came to us* through the leadership of the region. We had to *take these instructions to the branches*; *the branches had to take it to the area committees and the area committees had to take it to the street committees.*[28]

At the same time, the plan had important features promoting local initiative and participation. This can be seen in how Mandela elaborated on the aims, again showing the approach to be quite different from a 'vanguardist' one: 'to build up in the local branches themselves local Congresses which will effectively represent the strength and will of the people; ... to extend and strengthen the ties between Congress and the people and to consolidate Congress leadership.'[29] Its popular character is spelt out in Mandela's autobiography, where he mentions secret meetings with a number of ANC and SAIC leaders, some of whom were banned, to discuss the parameters of the plan. After this consultation, Mandela developed a system broad enough to allow for local conditions and not 'fetter individual initiatives', but sufficiently detailed to ensure order:

> The smallest unit was the cell, which in urban townships consisted of roughly ten houses on a street. A cell steward would be in charge of each of these units. If a street had more than ten houses, a street steward would take charge and the cell stewards would report to him. A group of streets formed a zone directed by a chief steward, who was in turn responsible to the secretariat of the local branch of the ANC. The secretariat was a subcommittee of the branch executive, which reported to the provincial secretary. My notion was that every cell and street steward should know every person and family in his area, so that he would be trusted by the people and would know whom to trust. The cell steward arranged meetings, organised political classes and collected dues. He was the linchpin of the plan. Although the strategy was primarily created for predominantly urban areas, it could be adapted to rural ones. [30]

The cell stewards needed to be a source of intelligence, knowing what was happening in every street. They had to know of social events, for the ANC often used these to advance its goals. They had a security function, knowing who were policemen, and who could act when the ANC intended infringing any particular regulation.[31]

The concept 'steward' appears to come not from its present association primarily with trade unions but from the function within the Methodist Church of 'material custodian in church affairs'. Not only was Methodism a significant feeder of the trade union movement in Britain, where the role of the shop steward evolved, but it was the church to which perhaps the majority of church-going Africans belonged, especially in the Eastern Cape, where Methodist missions had a long and deep hold.[32] Here once again is evidence of the continuities between very different phases in the history of African nationalism. While Christianity was not directly involved in the ANC of the 1950s, Christianity and Christian organisation in various forms had played a key part in influencing the formation of African nationalism when it began.[33]

One of the ironies of the M-Plan is that it subverted Nationalist government plans for imposing political control through the building of townships for Africans in the 'white' cities. Joe Matthews makes the point:

> Obviously it was a serious weakness in terms of rural organisation. It assumed funnily enough the classic township planning so you actually went to the city council and said, 'Can we have a copy of your township plan?' and you took the township plan and you divided the area, and you had the streets all there and it was quite easy to do it, following the traditional Verwoerd-type organisation, concentration of a township. And I think it was utilising that which had been intended as a security measure, to have townships far from the white areas and which then was turned around and made to be an advantage to the movement, so you had the people not as prisoners of the regime but as people organised in certain strategic areas. And of course in the end people in places like Soweto and so on when they got organised later in the '70s and the '80s, this was the system that was used.[34]

◎

In motivating the plan, and indeed throughout the 1950s, considerable stress was put on political education.[35] Many people appear to have gone through some form of internal education where a common understanding of Congress policies and ideology was developed in lectures and discussion. Those who participated at one level were expected to give the lectures at another.[36] Such processes were already in operation within the trade union movement, notably in Natal.[37]

The ANC introduced an elementary political education course for standardised use throughout the country. The aim was not only to build political understanding but to maintain organisational cohesion. Lectures were given secretly by branch leaders, but it was intended that the audience would over time deliver them to others, which they did. After a while this developed into a set curriculum. There were three courses: 'The World We Live In', 'How We Are Governed', and 'The Need for Change'. The lecturers were mainly banned individuals, enabling them to avoid falling into passivity and also keeping them in touch with the membership.[38]

Inside and outside these usually small units, many cadres saw political education as their key task during this period. Elias Motsoaledi, later to be a Rivonia trialist, from a very poor peasant background saw political education as giving impetus to the movement, with members who were not merely floating in an unconnected way; as he put it, this was having 'real members not only paper members'. People had to be taught the history of the ANC and understand the issues affecting them on a day-to-day basis.

> I had so many people from all over Soweto who came to me for political classes. I remember trying to impart this knowledge to someone who was far older than I was. I outlined the difficulties and then he looked at me and said, 'This is what I wanted to tell you, you can't tell me that.' In other words, you struck the chord and gained the respect of these people because you were able to interpret their aspirations. You were able to articulate all their problems. Then they started to respect you.'[39]

Through this kind of political education, members were not only inducted into the Congress movement but in some cases they developed into intellectuals. Gramsci uses the term for people who might not be formally trained but who perform a particular role in relation to others.[40] Many of these people had little, if any, formal education, yet they carried out an intellectual function. This was the case with Elias Motsoaledi; one informant told me that it was only when he got into exile that he realised that Motsoaledi was not 'an academician'.[41] A similar process had happened or would happen elsewhere – in the Communist Party in its early night schools and in the underground, in the MK camps, in trade unions, on Robben Island and in the UDF.

Throughout various phases of the South African struggle, internal courses had people learning one day and becoming teachers later on.[42]

One significant aspect of this political education, and certainly the courses, is that they were strongly Marxist,[43] with a pro-Soviet flavour. Generally, the widespread diffusion of Marxist thinking within the ANC until recently tends to be attributed to the exile experience, where some cadres were sent to Party schools and much of the political education was Marxist-oriented.[44] But these Congress Alliance courses indicate the existence and propagation of modes of analysis within that paradigm long before the period of exile.

Accounts of the early implementation of the M-Plan generally refer to it succeeding mainly in the Eastern Cape, particularly in Port Elizabeth.[45] But there are references to attempts in Cato Manor and even the whole of Durban (according to Eric Mtshali) as well as to East London and the Western Cape (Archie Sibeko).[46] John Nkadimeng also claims that the development of the M-Plan soon after its creation (as well as after 1960) was much wider than the areas conventionally named.[47] He insists that it was used in a number of areas of the then Transvaal, and that it had had some role in the Pondoland and Sekhukhuneland risings.[48] This claim, however, needs further investigation and clarification.

Nevertheless, the vision of countrywide coverage was not being achieved. By 1955 even the ANC's National Executive Committee pointed to the general failure to put the M-Plan in place:

> The National Liberation Movement has not yet succeeded in the organisational field in moving out of the domain of mass meetings and this type of agitation. Mass gatherings and large public activities of Congress are important, but so is house-to-house work, the building of small local branches and the close contact with members and supporters and their continual education.[49]

But the success of the M-Plan should not be measured just by how well it was implemented at the start, as Karis and Gerhart do.[50] This reaction may partly account for confusion or disagreement over its degree of success. In hindsight, it seems that it was used to a varying extent over the period immediately following its unveiling and then again later, after the banning of the ANC.

For various reasons – lack of resources, resistance to changes that did not seem immediately necessary, and fears of centralisation – many members were reluctant to make the organisational shift from open meetings at the time.[51] Also, as Joe Matthews indicated, when the M-Plan was being developed, banning and increased repression appeared imminent. But this did not last and the country returned to some semblance of normality, and many did not think it necessary to take the precautions when an immediate clampdown did not happen. This recalls Moses Kotane's statement when asked why the Communist Party had not prepared for underground before its banning. Kotane did not favour dissolution; but neither did he think it possible to have organised an illegal party before the Suppression of Communism Act became law.

> 'It is very easy to say we should,' he said later. 'But no person can react to nonexistent conditions. Many romantic people say we could have made preparations, but I dispute this. You don't walk looking over your shoulder when there is nothing to look back at. Theoretically you can train people to be pilots when there are no aeroplanes. But the realities have to be there.'[52]

In the same way, many ANC people may have found it too abstract to organise for illegality while the movement was still unbanned.[53] Once it was declared illegal, though, clandestine organisation became a necessity.

◎

Even if unevenly implemented in the early days, the M-Plan does seem to have become embedded in people's consciousness and formed the basis for organising underground units after 1960.[54]

A clear directive to implement the M-Plan was issued by the ANC Lobatse conference held in the then Bechuanaland in 1962.[55] The final resolutions instructed all organs and units 'as a matter of urgency ... to ensure the full implementation of the "M-plan" ... and its rapid extension to every area in South Africa; for this purpose to appoint special organisers to guide and supervise its operation.'[56]

Noloyiso Gasa describes what she saw, partly through the activities of her parents Vulindlela and Dorothy Zihlangu, who were leading ANC figures in the Western Cape, and her own experience of how the M-Plan was introduced after the ANC was banned. People were told not to meet in large numbers. She had enjoyed the general meetings, but was told that 'the securities have forced people not to meet in large numbers again. But we could see that people were meeting and you would gather from them that there was a plan that was proposed that people should meet in tens in separate venues.'[57]

While her parents saw themselves conforming to the M-Plan especially after the banning, they, like many others, carried habits of legality into the period of illegality – for example, storing membership records and keeping minutes of meetings. In the history of the ANC, achieving a system of records and minute-taking was a hard-won achievement from the 1940s. It was difficult for many to accept that this was a quality that was not only of little value but dangerous in the new situation. It is a consistent theme in liberation history that qualities or understandings that have been acquired through hard, dedicated work are not easily dispensed with. It was not easy for ordinary people, often with limited education, to learn to take minutes and keep records. Having acquired these habits and skills they tended to persist in situations where they were inappropriate. Equally the embryo of something new can often be detected in symptoms that by virtue of the rigid compartmentalisations imposed by historiographic periodisation have not been given adequate weight. We should observe both the symptoms and the legacies of the old, because both affect what is done later.

Similar practices can be found elsewhere. Photographs taken by Nat Serache in Dinokana, a village outside Zeerust in the then Western Transvaal, show a woman indicating where she used to hide ANC membership cards during the period of banning. Many members wanted to keep their cards in some safe place. When Ben Turok was canvassing for the Congress of the People in 1954, he encountered members of the former CPSA who had buried their cards in a tin box with plastic around it.[58] These mementoes or records were possibly a symbol of their continuing commitment to the organisation.

Frances Baard, speaking of Port Elizabeth, confirms that she understood the M-Plan as forming the basis for underground organisation in conditions of illegality. She speaks of there being about ten people in each cell and 'we were all from one place, one street and so forth.' There were only small group meetings, never big ones.[59]

In the early 1960s, underground units formed at Fort Hare were also organised according to the M-Plan. Isaac Mabindisa relates how they followed the plan and 'wouldn't meet in big groups, but in small groups. We would divide ourselves into cells.' Ntombi Dwane says that 'there was a hierarchy and your own connection was with your leader, your cell leader … There were about four of us in our cell … We'd have political discussions … We've got to do this now, we've got to go and scatter pamphlets, try and recruit a person, try and get somebody interested.'[60]

◎

When the ANC was banned in 1960, many of its leaders were already held together in prison under the State of Emergency. A meeting of the ANC National Executive was held – by those outside prison – where the decision was taken to declare a day of mourning.[61] On 1 April 1960 a statement issued by the Emergency Committee of the African National Congress, chaired by Moses Kotane, declared the ANC's intention to continue to give leadership and organisation to the popular struggle.

> The attempt to ban the African National Congress, which for half a century has been the voice of the voteless African majority in this country, is a desperate act of folly, committed by a Parliament which does not contain a single African.
>
> We do not recognise the validity of this law, and we shall not submit to it. The African National Congress will carry on in its own name to give leadership and organisation to our people until freedom has been won and every trace of the scourge of racial discrimination has been banished from our country.[62]

The new situation of illegality presented a challenge to those who had escaped arrest. The ANC's mode of organisation and structures had to be changed to meet the new situation. Michael Dingake describes the atmosphere of the time:

> While there had to be coordination at all levels, normal procedures and practices including democratic elections had to be suspended, replaced

by hierarchical appointments. The years of aboveground existence and the State of Emergency having removed some of the more experienced cadres made the task more difficult, especially with the morale of the ANC's mass constituency 'ailing'. [63]

Many of the members, however, found it hard to adapt to the transition. Dingake remembered the difficulty in communicating with and coordinating the membership. There was much confusion and even loyal members, lacking contact and guidance, 'swayed with the wind'.[64]

Some demoralisation and confusion was induced by the State of Emergency. The ANC had to contend with two forms of attrition at this time. On the one hand, a number of organisations which had not been banned or which claimed to represent black people tried to fill the vacuum left by the banning and take advantage of the ANC's banning. On the other, some people joined other organisations like the Liberal Party. Ian Mkhize, a former member of the Pietermaritzburg ANC branch, recalls:

> When the screws really did turn on the ANC, people were just nowhere to be found. I must say, it seemed for a while that the ANC had a demise – it seemed like it was virtually dead ... It was in 1963 that I joined the Liberal Party ... They were the only alternative that was available ... Somehow we had to get a political platform.[65]

Dingake comments on this trend, reading it possibly over-optimistically as indicating no sense of disillusionment with the ANC but focusing on the special qualities required, demands made and dangers faced in working underground and breaking from existing organisational habits.[66]

Cleopas Ndlovu also said it was hard to persuade branch members to recognise the changed situation. Many were reluctant to stop wearing Congress uniforms and to accept that what had been their legal rights were no more. Despite the tendency to retain habits of legality, in his experience substantial numbers went on to work in the underground organisation. He thought that they amounted to about sixty per cent of the membership of the branches he knew.[67] We cannot check such estimates; there is simply no way to verify the figure even for the branches familiar to Ndlovu.

Unlike the SACP, the ANC had not made serious, systematic preparations for working underground. Many of its members, as we have seen, could not relate to the notion in the abstract and hence were reluctant to make the necessary plans. While the SACP had not prepared adequately for illegality when it was banned in 1950 and dissolved itself amid much disarray, its reconstitution as an underground force was a gradual and carefully considered process. The ANC had taken some of the first steps. From the early 1950s, as we saw, many people felt that banning was inevitable sometime. The M-Plan was initiated to prepare for this, but it was not put in place on a wide geographical scale. Many writers may underestimate how far the plan was operational, but it is true that it was partial and very uneven in its impact. The moment of banning found the ANC unprepared on the whole.

After 1960 the M-Plan was the basis on which the ANC organised itself underground. But successful transition of a mass movement to an underground body was much more complicated than merely having a plan. Here, the expertise, facilities and active involvement of the SACP appear to have been crucial. The ANC drew upon them to develop its own covert capacity. By the time the ANC was banned the SACP had already had some seven years of experience underground. Many of the leading figures in the ANC underground were also members of the Communist underground organisation. All but one of the Rivonia accused are now known to have been members of the SACP, most of them in the leadership of the ANC.[68] Without the organisational muscle of the SACP, the ANC underground would have taken off with much greater difficulty.[69]

Yet some suspicion was felt towards the Communists. While Mtshali says that ANC comrades generally found it difficult to adapt to underground conditions, many left the ANC for that reason or because they suspected that 'it was the Communist Party doing work.'[70] But while the ANC and SACP sometimes shared facilities, as was the case at Rivonia, there was never a merger of the ANC and SACP underground. The SACP retained its vanguard and tightly knit, small-scale character.[71] Being a vanguard was not how the ANC saw itself, even underground. The ANC had the much more complex and difficult task of taking a mass, above-ground organisation below the surface.[72] Obviously this did not mean that every ANC member joined an underground unit. But the scale on which this occurred was much greater than in the case of the SACP and the security consequences were more problematic for the ANC.

The main task of the ANC underground immediately after the banning in 1960 appears to have been ensuring survival of the ANC as an organisation under completely new conditions of illegality. As long as the ANC was illegal it had to try to exert influence both from the underground and also through bodies that were still legal.

In Durban, Eric Mtshali relates how the South African Congress of Trade Unions (SACTU) continued to function legally, though many of its members had been detained or restricted. The space it occupied was used partly by the ANC to provide a platform for advancing its positions, along with SACP support. Mtshali reports: 'The Party's big task was . . . doing ANC work, [supporting] the ANC branches, using our experiences to build the ANC underground, also using SACTU, because SACTU was not banned and the leadership of SACTU were mainly Communists in almost all provinces.'[73]

Mtshali stressed the need to ensure survival of the ANC, and the basis for doing so was through implementing the M-Plan. Mtshali also recalls how the ANC in Natal tried to influence the direction of Residents' Associations. They had to 'work with them and say the same things that we were saying when we were ANC. But this time not as ANC but as members of the Residents' Associations and Ratepayers' Associations or as members of the unions.'[74]

Much of the work of the underground structures was on welfare: finding and providing aid to relatives of detainees, and organising legal defence and paying fines for those charged. This would continue to be one of the clandestine ANC roles, alongside the building of organisational structures, throughout most of the period underground. The covert structures facilitated recruitment to MK, including exit from and entry into the country for MK soldiers.[75]

The ANC underground was established almost at the same time that MK was formed, although the first operations of MK only took place a year later. Setting up MK as an organisation independent of the ANC represented a compromise which, Joe Matthews claims, created its own problems. Being outside the constitutional structures meant that the normal checks on who was recruited did not exist and that MK acted on its own, which sometimes led to serious security problems. Yet Cleopas Ndlovu insists that this is 'nonsense' and that ANC structures were involved in MK.[76] As he sees it, Matthews was not close to what was taking place because he was based in Basutoland (now Lesotho) at the time. This question deserves further investigation, since the potential for the problems that Matthews claims did occur must have been present if MK was independent of ANC structures.[77] If problems did arise, they may well have been related to the extent to which a *de facto* overlap existed between ANC and MK structures.

After a shaky start the ANC underground started to function, consolidating its organisational apparatus and work. Those who were in both ANC and MK say that MK performed well. According to Michael Dingake, its call for volunteers led to an unprecedented response from the youth, the organisation being 'inundated' with applications for training abroad.[78] But there were also serious lapses of security:

> The successful sabotage operations of 1962–3 created extreme overconfidence with its dangerous corollaries of recklessness and complacency. Regions, areas, streets and cells, through their structures, exhorted the membership to observe some elementary rules of security: change venues of meetings, be punctual at meetings, don't discuss your role in the organisation with other members of the organisation who are not working directly with you, be careful whom you talk to and what you say, etc. These elementary principles were broken daily . . . The optimistic side of the mood was good. The incipient complacency and recklessness produced by such a mood, however, was dangerous.[79]

Important logistical measures such as the transport of MK recruits out of the country were not always undertaken with due caution, as when drivers shouted on the streets that they would be making the journey.[80] On other occasions, MK recruits would be imposed, unscheduled, on cadres for accommodation, endangering a wide range of people.[81]

As a member of the Border Regional Command Secretariat, Sobizana Mngqikana was there at one point when more seasoned revolutionaries intervened, bringing comrades to heel. The Border committee had written demanding a report-back on the ANC conference in Lobatse without sensitivity to the changed conditions. In response, a delegation comprising Vuyisile Mini (one of the first three MK soldiers to be hanged, in 1964) and Caleb Mayekiso came to East London and chided the comrades there for their action: in affirming the importance of constitutional report-backs the East London comrades did not appear to place sufficient weight on the gravity of the new situation of armed struggle, where many lives would be lost.[82] The local comrades learnt the lesson, but sadly it did not spread more generally through the ranks.

Mngqikana, while a student at Fort Hare, painted defiant slogans and helped with anti-Republic activities. Returning to his home city, East London, he was recruited into an ANC underground structure:

> On reflection our East London underground . . . flouted most of the pertinent rules of conspiracy and clandestine work. And this inevitably was to lead to calamitous disaster, as we were to witness. For example, one of our leaders would boast to some non-ANC acquaintances that he had been reinforced by intellectuals in his [ANC] organisation. This meant us ex-Fort Hareians. We would be confronted by individuals claiming to know our political affiliations and activities. Sometimes we felt honoured by this, not appreciating the grave consequences that could arise. Sometimes we had fundraising parties where freedom songs were sung.[83]

The period that followed was one where the top ANC leadership was either imprisoned or avoided arrest through crossing borders into exile. The ANC was no longer a mass organisation, even if it might have continued to enjoy an extensive following whose presence would only re-emerge later. It would take almost thirty years before the ANC could resume the task of re-establishing itself on legal terrain with structures functioning at every level.

In the meantime, the organisation found itself in disarray, its leaders and members scattered in exile, prisons and various places inside the country, mainly with little apparent political content to their lives. While this apparent organisational absence was partly illusory, it gave confidence to the Nationalist regime that it had dealt a devastating blow.

◎

Academic literature sees the M-Plan as petering out in the 1950s after some success mainly in the Eastern Cape. The broader question being asked here is in what ways it helped to form the ANC underground later on in a number of parts of the country. As late as the 1980s it was the basis for organisation in Matatiele, an important sphere for ANC underground activity.[84] Activists in the Northern Transvaal also claimed that it helped them during the 1980s,[85] though the extent to which their approach coincided with the plan as originally conceived is not clear.

This chapter has also suggested that the 1950s was not only a period of popular protest but one where top-down transmission, hierarchical organisation and widespread diffusion of Marxist doctrine took place within the ANC. The tendency to contrast the exile experience with the allegedly more democratic and grassroots phases of the 1950s and 1980s has led some to ignore the presence of similar organisational characteristics found throughout the ANC's history after 1950, in varying degrees. It may be more true to see every phase after the 1950s as containing more or less both democratic and undemocratic elements, hierarchical and 'bottom-up' features, and that none deserves romanticising or any form of blanket characterisation.

Chapter 1 referred to the artificiality of rigid attempts to periodise ANC history. A constant theme of the present chapter is that some people enunciated and implemented a policy to fit the times while others stuck with old policy or acting out of future policies. This seems to be a relatively persistent feature of ANC history. A problem with the standard view of discrete phases in the ANC's struggle is that it tends to fetishise continuities or ruptures, while every period contains both. This was all too clear in the case where some people still wanted to wear ANC uniforms after the organisation was declared illegal. Other chapters will show how some jumped the gun in anticipating armed struggle just when the legality of the ANC was crucial to its public stance. The genesis of particular forms long before they are publicly announced and the persistence of old modes of operation after they are supposed to have stopped, both have their impacts, which require further interrogation.

It is true that the ANC was not adequately prepared for underground activity in 1960 and also that it operated under very disadvantageous conditions. In characterising these early efforts we need to understand that Africans had not had legal access to arms or military training throughout the period since Union in 1910, and that (unlike the SACP) the ANC attempted to take the entire membership underground. Everything was done under the pressure of each person being one day a legal operative and the next an outlaw. We can easily criticise recklessness and other problems in that situation, but it was also a fact that the leadership did not have the time to train cadres, who were therefore not adequately prepared to sustain an underground presence, especially as it was quite easy for the police to forecast who would join the units.

3

THE RECONSTITUTION OF THE SACP AS AN UNDERGROUND ORGANISATION

In 1953 the Communist Party of South Africa (CPSA), which had been proscribed by the Nationalist government three years earlier, was formally reconstituted as an underground organisation, the South African Communist Party, or SACP. It is a subject about which little is known. What we do know also tends to be urban and big city-biased; consequently it reflects the 'mainstream' Marxism of the central leadership, based primarily in Cape Town and Johannesburg, and tends to neglect the hybrid mixes between African belief systems and Marxism found for example in the former Northern Transvaal, where a Central Committee member, Flag Boshielo, was also a spiritual healer.[1] The type of communism understood in some of these rural areas may thus have diverged significantly from the 'mainstream' urban conception. Some of the leaders mixed Marxism with African belief systems and practices, notably Boshielo and Elias Motsoaledi, and it is by no means clear whether it was the African or the Marxist that formed the foundation in their bodies of thinking. The account that follows may therefore neglect important parts of the story which have not yet been recorded and for which sources are fast disappearing.

The Communist underground, throughout its history, made a substantial contribution towards developing the ANC-led underground, sometimes disproportionate to the number of Party members involved. The manner in which that contribution was made left its mark on the relationship between the Party and the ANC. Contrary to the fairly common view that the ANC underground was dominated by Communists, the relationship was more complex and may even have limited the extent to which the SACP itself was able to act as an independent force.

◎

Within two years of the National Party coming to power in 1950, it had prepared legislation to outlaw the CPSA. Before this was enacted, the Party's Central Committee (CC) met in an emergency session. It considered several options. The first was to 'do nothing and wait for the curtain to fall'; but legal advice had it that any member who could not prove to have resigned would become liable for criminal prosecution. The second option was to claim to have dissolved and then to reconstitute the party secretly as an underground movement; but the majority of members decided against this 'partly because almost all our members were known to the police, had no experience of underground ways of work, and would therefore have little chance of underground survival. It would be a defiant gesture but no more, with extremely serious consequences. The CC was not prepared to take responsibility for that either.'[2]

Rusty Bernstein, a former leading member, suggests that the Party's history until then had largely been concerned with safeguarding its own legality and constitutional rights, and that 'forty years of legality had coated its revolutionary edge with fat, and principle had been overtaken by pragmatism. By the time the CC met to see to its defences they had already fallen into disuse. It had clutched at the "legal opinion" like a drowning man at a straw.'[3]

Members had awaited the CC statement with some anxiety, wanting direction on what they would do next. Added to this was the pervasive atmosphere of fear, the threat that the state would act punitively against Party members and that the Party would suffer the same fate that had befallen the German Communist Party under Nazi rule. By this was meant on the one hand a fear of concentration camps but, at a practical level, the appreciation of difficulty in swift, almost uninterrupted transition from being a legal organisation to having underground modes of organisation.[4] In the end, with two dissenting votes, the decision was taken to dissolve.

The announcement is described by Bernstein as akin to a 'communiqué from headquarters':

[Moses] Kotane [General Secretary of the Party] added a few low-key words of regret, and sat down. The meeting sat silent, stunned. We had been speculating about what we might hear, but no one had anticipated it would be no more than hail and farewell … We had come expecting a message of courage, hope, perhaps defiance or confrontation; but not cold surrender without a whimper.[5]

Like Bernstein, many Party members greeted the dissolution with disbelief and dismay. Some thought it was merely a ruse and that the real intention was immediately to regroup as an underground organisation.[6] But this was not the plan. It was a decision that would later be severely criticised by members as a weakness and error on the part of its leaders, who had not consulted the rank and file. Once taken, though, it had profound effects on the history of the Party.[7]

◎

According to some commentators, the decision whether to dissolve outright or re-form reflected regional biases. Capetonians, who dominated the CC, appeared reconciled to dissolution, while the suggestion to take steps towards preparing for underground organisation came from the Transvaal.[8] Likewise, after the dissolution, CC members had diverse understandings of their future role. While some saw dissolution as a final step, for others it was a tactical manoeuvre.[9] According to Bunting, Moses Kotane, 'together with the majority of the Central Committee members, automatically assumed that after the formal act of dissolution, the Central Committee would begin to reconstitute the Party on new lines suited to the illegal conditions.'[10] But some of the leadership and membership were not prepared to join an illegal organisation – and there were others, like Ismail Meer, who were not invited to join once the Party was in fact reconstituted.[11] Given the new conditions required for operation, many of those who had been members in the period of legality were not considered suited to illegal work.[12] Among those who refused to join the underground SACP were the chair of the Party at the time of its dissolution, Ike Horvitch, and the leading theoretician, Jack Simons, although his wife, Ray Alexander, did. Alexander describes how Brian Bunting came to ask them to join the underground Party and she immediately accepted, but Jack walked out of the room and later berated her for not first discussing it privately with him.[13] Jack Simons only rejoined the Party over twenty years later. According to Bunting, Simons's decision was not ideological but based on family considerations. He assumed that Ray Alexander would face arrest, and one parent was needed in the house.[14] But his non-involvement shocked many, for, as Ahmed Kathrada says, Simons was regarded as a 'hero'.[15]

Apart from questions of capacity to adapt to conditions of illegality, the decision whether to join the reconstituted Party or not turned, it has been argued, on different perspectives about the relationship between class and national struggle, and in particular on the validity in the South African context of the theory of 'colonialism of a special type'.[16] This theoretical approach, which was adopted by both the SACP in 1962 and later the ANC from the late 1960s, was an attempt to characterise South African society by linking the key concepts of both race and class, or national oppression and class exploitation, in its analysis. From this approach flowed certain strategies and tactics which differed from the prevailing emphasis on either race or class, and instead emphasised their combined effect. [17]

The theory saw apartheid South Africa as representing a distinct variant of capitalist rule and of colonialism. Its distinction lay in that the essential features of colonial domination persisted and were even intensified after the Act of Union in 1910. This was especially manifested by the whites, who were characterised as 'colonisers', and the 'oppressed colonial majority' being located within a single country. In such a system, power and wealth were overwhelmingly concentrated in the hands of whites while denial of human rights and political oppression created conditions for super-exploitation of labour power and oppression of all black people 'nationally', as a people. The process did not have a uniform effect in that there were differential benefits derived among whites, and a range of impacts of oppression experienced by black people, with class differentials in each case.[18]

As with the decision to dissolve, adherence or otherwise to the theory of 'colonialism of a special type' may have had a regional bias, with those in the Cape allegedly being less sympathetic to the national struggle. Fred Carneson, former Cape CPSA secretary, has commented:

Until the African National Congress, or the Congress movement, emerged as a real political force in South Africa, I think there was a tendency among the activists inside and outside the Party to see things in class terms more than in national liberatory terms. Particularly so, I think, amongst some of the white communists, though it was not confined to the white communists by any manner of means.[19]

However, Bunting denies this claim of ideological differences.[20]

The reference to the ANC as a 'real political force' is important. For most of the Party's existence the ANC had been very weak organisationally and its activities mainly revolved around its annual conference. It was only under the secretary-generalship of the Revd James Calata and the presidency of Dr AB Xuma that attempts were made to turn the ANC into an organised force. This created a foundation for the later emergence of the Youth League (YL) and the implementation of its plans in the ANC's Programme of Action, thus turning the ANC into a mass force in the 1950s.[21] Despite the initial anti-Communist flavour of YL pronouncements, the turn to mass politics was one of the factors creating a base for an alliance between the SACP and the ANC as the key components of the national liberation movement.

The centrality of the theory of 'colonialism of a special type' in the reconstitution of the Communist Party, and decisions on whether or not to participate, may be debatable. This was nevertheless a significant moment in that the clear elaboration of a mode of analysis accommodating both national liberation and a long-term commitment to socialism facilitated the development of a Communist–ANC alliance.

Establishing an underground organisation was a task filled with difficulty, but there were some factors that aided the process. We have seen in the previous chapter that some Communists had been trained in and had limited experience in underground work. While this was not the same as organisational preparation, many of the individuals concerned would become important in the establishment of an underground Communist Party.

Probably more important was that some time had elapsed between the dissolution of the CPSA and the moment of establishment of the SACP, which allowed Communists to become actively involved in other political activities such as the various Congresses – the ANC, the South African Indian Congress (SAIC), and later the South African Congress of Trade Unions (SACTU), on which the Security Police focused their attention. The existence of these organisations enabled Communists to be present but not visible *as Communists*. Monitoring those non-SACP activities determined the focus of the police and may have left them absorbed with Communist influence in the various Congresses rather than considering the possibility of the reconstitution of the Party itself. No overall strategic intelligence capacity existed in the state which might have envisaged the re-establishment of the Party. The intelligence capacity on domestic affairs then was in any case limited to the initially inept efforts of the Special Branch of the South African Police. Police intelligence (not just in South Africa, where it may have been especially weak) is inherently unsuited to such a task, in that it is by its nature operational, aimed at apprehending offenders rather than considering broader strategic questions, a capacity that would start to develop later, especially in the National Intelligence Service under Dr Niel Barnard.[22]

What is more, the dissolution of the CPSA and its apparent continued organisational absence created a sense of complacency on the side of the authorities. That the Party was relatively invisible in the sense of having no public profile until 1960, even from underground, would also have reduced police attention and made detection more difficult.

In the process of reconstituting the Party under a new name in 1953, great care and numerous precautions were observed. In conditions of utmost secrecy, a small working group of senior figures began to reconstitute the Party, building up a new network of units, also called cells (the terminology varied). 'Their numbers were small – fewer than 100 members were at the core of Communist Party activity, most of them living in the Transvaal. They operated mainly in small units of four or five people, meeting clandestinely, often in "unmarked" cars owned by friends and colleagues or in "safe" houses.'[23]

According to Bunting, Kotane and most of his comrades immediately set about reconnecting with individuals to develop plans for re-establishing the Party. Kotane was under close surveillance and had no headquarters from which to operate, meetings having to be held at early hours often in the open veld away from the big cities, sometimes behind bushes where they would be unobserved but from where they could detect any unwanted presence. Arrangements for every meeting would be made in advance, with the exact time and spot where each individual would be collected and dropped, set down in advance. No regular pattern was allowed to develop. Where transport was by car, these had to be changed regularly, and places and personnel had to be constantly altered. No one should observe any routine type of gathering. All written communication was avoided.

An arduous process leading to the formation of the first groups was followed in Cape Town, sometimes in houses and sometimes on the slopes of Table Mountain or in the thickets of the Cape Flats. Similar groups were established in Durban and Port Elizabeth and other areas, and Kotane sent couriers to each centre to ascertain what was being done and establish communication links. Building secret organisation in a secure manner was a slow task, 'but Kotane insisted from the start that security was to be of the tightest, and personally checked on every detail.'[24]

The first task was obviously to ensure that reconstitution was sustainable, that structures created would endure whatever pressures might arise. Recruitment was undertaken on a very careful and conservative basis. Someone might recommend a person and, if found to be suitable, he or she would be recruited and placed in a unit by someone else. The process of vetting was 'very strict'.

> The unit would say well this is 'a potential'. It would not recruit him, but what the unit could do is if it is running some broader classes it could invite that person there, not letting him or her know it is a Communist Party thing.
>
> The Communists would be watching who the 'potentials' were and the unit would then say that we think we should recommend A, B, and C. The District Committee would then go through very carefully and decide, and the recruitment would take place; but, depending on where the person is going to be placed eventually, then someone from that unit would then approach that person.[25]

The trade unions were fertile ground for the underground Party and they would watch how people conducted themselves and identify who could be potentially recruited.

People would observe simple, elementary rules of behaving and operating, which, even though they were similar to techniques found in detective novels, proved adequate for secure functioning. People continued the earlier tight security – never travelling together when attending meetings, and documents were seldom if ever carried to meetings; if needed for discussion, they would be destroyed there. Members often did not know the venue beforehand and arrangements were put in place that made this unnecessary, for example by collection at some prearranged point.

The Party was organised at three levels: Central Committee, District Committees, and units, or cells. The last seldom comprised more than four people. In some cases it was considered more secure to segregate people and not mix white and black, since this could attract attention. In the Cape and Natal, however, mixed units appear to have been fairly common.

Members usually only knew those in the unit within which they worked, again by code names unless they already knew the person's real name, which was fairly common in so small a party, especially at leadership levels. At a District Committee level individuals would also interact with the units they coordinated, though the District Committee as a whole, while knowing the numbers involved, would not know the actual names of members in various units.

Not everyone was organised into a unit. A category of members known as 'D' (recalled by others as 'C' category) was safeguarded against exposure to the membership. Kathrada describes them as 'underground, underground Communists'. This was sometimes because they had no record of previous involvement in the Party and were very unlikely to arouse suspicion, amongst them being leading advocate Vernon Berrangé, QC.[26]

There were also people who were not members, including leading figures who contributed funds or interacted on a close basis with Party members and leadership. According to Billy Nair, one such person was Dr Monty Naicker, non-Communist and leader of the Natal Indian Congress, who interacted with Nair and one or two others whom he knew to be Communists, and through whom he made his financial contributions. Others made facilities available to the Party for various types of meetings.[27] There are numerous cases of meetings in doctors' surgeries or conferences at the back of shops of Indian traders, who were not present at the time.[28]

Chief Albert Luthuli, well known as a non-Communist Christian, became very close to Moses Kotane during the Treason Trial, so much so that he never subsequently took any important decision without consulting Kotane, often bypassing other ANC officials in order to seek his counsel. Walter Sisulu recalls that before agreeing to any decisions Luthuli would ask, 'Does Moses Kotane know about this?'[29] Bunting quotes an interview with the late ANC President, Oliver Tambo:

> It is significant that Chief Luthuli, who was not a member of the Party, and not near to being a member, on difficult questions on which he wanted advice bypassed his officials and secretaries and sent for Moses because he had discerned his loyalty to him. He knew Moses was 100 percent a member of the Communist Party, in fact its general secretary; but he also knew him to be 100 per cent ANC, and this gave Luthuli great confidence in him. Even when Luthuli was confined to the Groutville area in Natal, he would send for Moses to explain or discuss some issue he was uncertain about.[30]

He also relied on people whom he knew to be Communists for logistical support on occasions when he broke his banning orders. From the time of the Treason Trial he also became an avid reader of Marxist and SACP literature. Special arrangements were made to deliver copies of the *African Communist* (at first published as an independent journal, but later to become the official organ of the SACP) to Luthuli in Groutville. This was in no way an indication that the chief was becoming a Marxist, but he had an enquiring mind and wanted to understand communism, which through the claim that the Freedom Charter aimed at establishing a dictatorship of the proletariat had been a prominent element in the state indictment in the Treason Trial.[31]

Quantitative growth of underground organisation necessitated mechanisms for democratic participation through which individual members could influence national policy. The SACP held a number of conferences during this period. As Kathrada recalls:

> The first conference took place at an Indian shop in the East Rand. There was a shop and a storeroom at the back. Now that Indian guy would have left for the weekend. Then there was a house too, I think, because we stayed there. All of us were taken there by car. All staying there for the weekend. On mattresses on the ground. It was not a very

posh house. Some must have slept in the storeroom. The shop was closed. That was the first conference. [32]

Slovo, making a veiled and, given its sensitivity, rather convoluted allusion to the recruitment of top ANC figures,[33] noted:

> Between 1952 and 1962 the Party had six underground conferences, and the last one, when the Party Programme was adopted after a thorough discussion in the underground units, recorded impressive achievements throughout the country after a decade of underground work. This conference was attended by delegates from every major urban centre and by historic figures whose relatively recent conversion to the cause of socialism and the Party was a positive sign that our roots were indeed spreading deeper in the indigenous soil.[34]

The conditions under which the Party was forced to operate obviously shaped the kind of internal politics that developed within it. Secretiveness is unconducive to critical debate, and conditions of danger made reading and discussion of unorthodox, more critical versions of Marxism a luxury that did not come into consideration. Very few of the leading Communists appear, from my experience, to have been regular readers of emerging 'New Left' critical perspectives in journals like *New Left Review, Review of African Political Economy* and similar places of debate, other than Joe Slovo, Ruth First and Harold Wolpe (and Wolpe became fairly inactive over the years).

The 1962 Programme made no bones about the curtailment of internal democracy entailed in working underground:

> The structure of the Party is based on the principles of democratic centralism. While demanding strict discipline, the subordination of a minority to the majority and of lower Party organs to higher organs, and the prohibition of all factions within the Party, it upholds the principle of democratic election of all leading organs of the Party, collective leadership and full debate of policy. The curtailment of some aspects of democratic procedure is inevitable under illegal conditions; this temporary situation must be compensated for by all members, regarding it as their duty to participate in the formulation of policy and by the leadership, encouraging and making it possible for them.[35]

Slovo likewise records that the demands of underground did not lead to the wiping out of internal democracy within the SACP:

> We continued to practise a good measure of internal Party democracy. The rank and file had the opportunity of debating major policy statements before they were finally adopted by the Central Committee. An election system was devised which was designed to achieve a balance between the often contradictory requirements of security and democracy.[36]

Joe Matthews agrees. He claims that ANC preparations for underground under the M-Plan were essentially undemocratic, but insists that the SACP underground operated on a democratic basis, always giving members the chance to discuss questions before decisions were taken.[37] If this was true, it may also have had something to do with the conditions under which each organisation prepared for underground and the relative stability and slower pace of the process in the case of the SACP.

The extent to which membership participated must have varied in different periods of illegality and the conditions of repression being experienced. Certainly, when the 1989 Party conference was held in Cuba, there was a great deal of input from within the country towards finalising the preparatory documents. This was also aided by the presence of then senior Party officials involved in Operation Vula, the attempt to return outside figures to join internal underground structures.[38]

⊚

Interviews with Party members suggest that the main tasks of the underground SACP were dedicated to building other Congresses (of which they were members) into stronger organisations, though independent Party units were established as the underground developed, especially in the 1980s. Precisely how their tasks were divided seems to have varied.

Kathrada recalls that the Party of the 1950s and 1960s dealt 'more with our work in the Congress movement'.[39] While some internal political education was conducted and new members were recruited, this work in the Congress movement – working to strengthen the ANC – would seem to have remained the prime emphasis of the Party throughout its period of illegality.

Despite the extent of involvement in Congress organisations, some SACP members were initially reluctant to join the ANC. Even after joining the SACP, Eric Mtshali was not a member of the ANC:

> I would attend ANC mass rallies. But I didn't find anything interesting. All I would hear [was] Fighting for Independence, which was to me far away. It did not answer my immediate problems, which were bread and butter issues, higher wages and better working conditions. So to me those ANC mass rallies did not make much sense.[40]

At the same time members take pride in the SACP having initiated the 'main decisions' in the organisations or having been crucial to the resolution of problems in all the Congresses. Joe Matthews says:

> Remember, up to 1960 the Party did not announce its existence – although any intelligent person could have seen the coordination, not only in the Party but in the broad democratic movement. People spoke with one voice too often and it was obvious that there was a coordinating force. I must say that, contrary to popular belief, every important decision was taken by the Party, not by the ANC.[41]

Concern began to be felt within the SACP about Communists operating as a unified bloc within the Congresses. As a result, according to Dr Yusuf Dadoo, the SACP decided to change its strategy:

> Previously you would take decisions in the Party and go and implement them. That they said is no longer allowed. You can discuss but you don't take decisions and say this is a Party decision and we'll go to the Congress and try and push through a decision ... In other words, for the Communists in the past it was a rigid thing. You take a line, which you take to the Congresses and implement.[42]

Ben Turok refers to this interaction between the Communist Party and the Congress movement in the 1950s as 'obviously undemocratic'.[43] But one may reasonably ask if such a process, as Kathrada and Matthews have described it, is susceptible to so simple a characterisation. If people caucus and then put a position and win it democratically, that is not undemocratic.[44] It is what all like-minded people do in most organisations. This is not to ignore the problems that Kathrada refers to in Communists arriving with common positions. That is why Dadoo sought to stop it. But their intervention predetermined as a collective in order to secure a particular decision was not in itself undemocratic, by any manner of speaking.

We have seen the evidence of an overall Marxist content of Congress Alliance courses. Clearly, political education was a major arena of Communist input in the ANC-led liberation movement as a whole. The Party also distributed literature reflecting its position, but not initially under its own name (since the organisation had not itself emerged publicly), for example the publication *Inkululeko* ('Freedom'), later the name of an underground Party journal in the 1970s.

The Party's close interaction with the Congresses was also aimed at identifying potential SACP recruits. SACTU used to hold large meetings and debates in Durban. Nair describes how they would identify from these discussions who could perhaps be drawn into the Party.[45]

As we have seen in Chapter 2, the reconstitution of the Communist Party had importance for the later development of the ANC as an underground organisation. The ANC drew on the considerable experience and some of the facilities of the SACP in developing its own organisational capacity underground.

Almost simultaneously with the process of establishing an ANC underground, MK was formed. The decision to take up arms arose first in the SACP, though there had been talk of 'fighting back' in various parts of the country throughout the 1950s.[46] Risings in Pondoland, Sekhukhuneland, and Natal and Zululand, and the burning of sugarcane fields, indicated, as Nelson Mandela was to observe at the Rivonia Trial, that unless the ANC took steps to control and regulate the drive towards violence it would lead to a catastrophe.

Although the SACP had initiated the idea of armed struggle, it knew that it could not be the driving force or organisation, especially given the need for support in Africa. An indication of the difficulties likely to be faced by Communists, especially non-African ones, was Joe Slovo later being declared a prohibited immigrant by the Tanzanian government, forcing him to relocate to London.[47]

After the Rivonia Trial, various ANC and SACP units remained at large for a few more years. However, with the sentencing of Bram Fischer in 1966, the Communist underground was effectively smashed. Yet the 'political dormancy', the silence that is referred to in much of the literature, does not reflect the almost immediate, albeit small-scale, attempts to reconstruct the organisation.

In the late 1960s and the 1970s, a number of Communist-initiated propaganda units were established within the country, often by recruiting people who had been studying overseas. Amongst these was Ahmed Timol, who was tortured to death in 1971. These units were responsible for distributing official publications of the SACP and also ANC, as well as sometimes producing other publications such as *Vukani! / Awake!*, written inside the country. Their lifespan tended to depend on the extent of their activity: the more they produced, the more likely the police were to detect the pattern of their work and close in on the unit. In general, none of these groups appear to have avoided capture for longer than four years, though there may have been some that were never arrested.

These were strictly propaganda units, with instructions not to do anything attracting attention to themselves, as would have happened in interracial units or open, progressive activity. The units tended to be racially exclusive, which conformed to the character of the time, in order that in so precarious an operation nothing should be done that would attract attention.

In the 1980s units were established with a more far-ranging character, producing both ANC and SACP literature, acting as both ANC and SACP units, and conducting a range of underground activities. This was the case in a number of provinces. Paul Mashatile in Alexandra Township, together with other members of the Alexandra Youth Congress executive, was drawn into underground work. Significantly, Mashatile's unit stored their materiel in one of the premises of a 'puppet' councillor, a supposed collaborator who was so despised by the community that his house was burnt down.[48]

A similar far-ranging contribution in the 1980s initially derived from informal groupings of Catholic youth who had been subjected to left-wing as well as ANC influences within the Church. The way in which members of units were inducted was a mixture of Marxist-Leninist teaching and ANC political education. Although it is not clear whether many or most were formal members of the SACP, their main links within the liberation movement were through Party members in Zimbabwe.[49]

During the pre-1976 period considerable activity took place, initiated outside the country, the most notable achievement being Chris Hani's pioneering and difficult entry into South Africa just after being elected Assistant General Secretary of the SACP in 1974. While Shubin is at great pains to assert that Hani was then in this SACP position, the extent to which Party or ANC could be said to have initiated a particular activity was often blurred. After his return from South Africa Hani established a base in Lesotho and repeatedly crossed into the country and helped build units. Structures were established in the Free State, Transkei, Western Cape, Eastern Cape and Border.[50]

It is not known how many people engaged at various times in underground struggle for the SACP. They clearly consisted of only a few hundred in the 1950s and early 1960s, but may have increased significantly in the preparation of MK people for underground work outside and inside the country from the mid-1970s and into the 1980s.

The joint ANC–SACP Operation Vula of the mid-1980s, coordinated by then ANC President Oliver Tambo and then SACP General Secretary Joe Slovo, envisaged a qualitative shift in the character of underground work, returning significant leadership figures into the country so that their interventions would not happen from a distance but on the spot. It was intended to merge internal and external underground organisation to a greater extent than before. Most of those who entered the country or participated in Vula activities appear to have been Communists then.[51] Following the unbanning of organisations in February 1990, this initiative was overtaken by events.

The establishment of the SACP underground took place at a time when the ANC–SACP alliance was consolidated and a common analysis of national democratic struggle was emerging. But what did the character of this alliance mean for the relative status of the two components and their independent character?

The conditions under which the Party emerged underground had some characteristics that may have left their mark on relations with the ANC throughout the period of illegality. Despite its reconstitution in 1953, it took seven years before the Party announced its independent existence, a decision which some figures like Moses Kotane and Yusuf Dadoo opposed, fearing it would compromise relations between the

ANC and the Party.[52] Some commentators confirm the hesitancy of Kotane and his resistance to destabilising the relationship of Communists within the ANC. The decision to emerge appears to have been taken by the small group of Central Committee members (its lack of representivity being one of Kotane's bases for objection) who were outside prison, and was met with mixed feelings.[53]

While the relationship between national and class struggle was subsequently formulated as coterminous, it seems that, for many, the 'two-stage theory' then prevalent was initially interpreted as meaning a concentration on building the national struggle and in particular its main vehicle, the ANC. To some extent there appears to have been reluctance about the Party speaking in its own name.

It also appears that this was the pattern in exile. Oliver Tambo initially expressed reservations about Party people meeting as separate units. He phrased his notions of the relationship between the two organisations in inclusive terms, not wanting to think of Party people as different from other ANC members.[54] This obviously would also tend to obliterate the independent character of the Party. This perspective of Tambo is well captured in interviews conducted by Bunting about the role of Kotane. Kotane's position was critical because he was the key individual in forging the ANC–SACP relationship:

> I think Moses Kotane contributed more than anyone to this kind of collaboration between the ANC and the Party, to the unification of the liberation movement in South Africa. He could have used his position to underline attitudes, which were specific to the Communist Party, to speak from a particular position and remind everybody about the ultimate objectives of the Communist Party. But he never did that. *He debated from what seemed to be an exclusive ANC standpoint*, and from the point of view of building unity this was extremely important. I am absolutely certain that many people who might have been hostile to the Party were won over because they found a man like Kotane to be an ANC man second to none.[55]

Tambo refers to no one being fooled by the dissolution of the Communist Party, knowing that Party members never ceased to be members and that the Party contributed to the development of progressive policies in the ANC.[56] Then: 'Before 1950 there was the feeling that there were two camps; some belonged to one, some to the other. But after 1950 we were all together and *when we discussed policies we never thought of the differences in our philosophies.* We were all equals deciding what must be done.'[57]

All together yes, but clearly it was under overall command of the ANC. When people were to be sent to the International Lenin School for studies, Tambo had to approve them. When Joe Slovo was chosen as General Secretary of the Party, Tambo's permission was required to release him from duties in the ANC, enabling him to take on that role.

Even in 1990, after the unbanning, the legacy of these ANC claims over Party officials was seen when the Party wanted Chris Hani to be Deputy General Secretary and released from his tasks in MK. The ANC was refusing to allow this and it was only when the Party conference of 1991 elected Hani General Secretary, without seeking permission, that this changed. According to Dipuo Mvelase, former MK camp commander and until recently deputy chair of the SACP, MK never forgave the Party for taking Hani away from MK because of the special concern which he had for soldiers.[58] This statement relates specifically to concerns for the welfare of soldiers, but also reflects a sense of ownership over Hani claimed by the ANC army, a prior claim that they sought to have prevail over that of the SACP.

There needs to be a more careful examination of SACP–ANC relations in the period of exile. Many top leaders were in fact also Party leaders at the time (though several allowed their membership to lapse in 1990). But the presence of large numbers of Party members in leadership structures of the ANC does not mean the Party was necessarily giving it strategic direction.

Certainly, key Party strategic interventions were made at some points in decision-making within the ANC, in particular the adoption of the theory of 'colonialism of a special type' by the ANC. But we need to ask whether, beyond that, the selection of top ANC cadres for Party membership was used to benefit specifically Party purposes, or whether it became primarily a Party presence within the ANC, carrying out almost purely ANC tasks.[59] Shubin refers to a Central Committee decision in the 1960s to set up Party organisations outside South Africa. The process was 'very slow', the main reason, apart from practical difficulties, being hesitation on the part of the leadership 'primarily by Moses Kotane'. Chris Hani, in an interview with Sonia

Bunting in May 1974, expressed his concerns:

> After coming out of prison [in Botswana, after retreating during the Wankie campaign in then Rhodesia] I made a serious attempt to organise Party life. I saw Moses was keen on preserving the cohesion of the national liberation movement. He realised there were enemies and he felt the Party should never give them the excuse to destroy the good working relations between the two organisations [the ANC and SACP]. Because of his credentials he felt that he himself was representing the Party in the ANC and that therefore there was no need for the Party itself. In a way he succeeded, he achieved the respect of OR [Oliver Reginald Tambo] and indirectly OR's recognition of the Party is mirrored in Moses. But Moses went too far.[60]

This is not to question the large measure of convergence between ANC and SACP goals, not only in a specific phase of the struggle but even potentially in a conceivable transition to socialism. This is clearly manifested in the 'Green Book', the report of a commission established after an ANC visit to Vietnam.[61] Part of the report states: 'It should be emphasised that no member of the Commission had any doubts about the ultimate need to continue our revolution towards a socialist order; the issue was posed only in relation to the tactical considerations of the present stage of our struggle.' The commission members and signatories were Oliver Tambo, Thabo Mbeki, Joe Slovo, Moses Mabhida, Joe Gqabi and Joe Modise. Callinicos remarks that Tambo 'obtained the agreement of Moses Mabhida [then General Secretary of the SACP] that the SACP existed to promote socialism. There was to be, therefore, no immediate subtext in the ANC's quest for broad, mass support.'[62] This is a strange conclusion. It was hardly a concession for the SACP to promote socialism, since it was already in their programme. The significant passage quoted above, about agreement that socialism was the ultimate goal, while not raising it then for 'tactical' reasons, is not mentioned. Surely that is a very important subtext?

The interrelationship between the ANC and SACP raises broader questions when the two independent organisations relating to one another in alliance are unequal, and the one is the leader of a liberation movement. But was there only one way that this could have unfolded, in which Party leaders were praised for being indistinguishable from ANC?

Could a Party presence have been manifested more independently?

A rather uncomfortable question needs to be asked: Did the Party allow itself to become a 'route to greatness'? In the exile period, the Party commanded various resources and networks through which people could have access to superior training and various opportunities for advancement. The Party was regarded as an 'elite' organisation. Because of the recognition that membership entailed, recruitment as a member of the Party could enhance the possibility of rising in various other structures, in MK and the ANC broadly.

In short, this had some of the characteristics of a patronage network. In such situations there was the temptation, for people who were able to do so, to take advantage of these resources and seek Party membership – as much for the benefits that accrued as for whatever ideological convictions were supposed to accompany them. We need to ask whether the post-1990 defections do not partially confirm this. None of those who withdrew cited ideological differences, and some claimed to have never been members.

Finally, all of this has recent significance. When Jabu Moleketi and Josiah Jele issued a long pamphlet filled with voluminous quotations from classic Marxist and Leninist texts, one of the objectives they declared was to advise that the Party remain the 'Party of Kotane'.[63] This pamphlet was distributed at a time when the SACP with COSATU, in the new conditions of the post-apartheid dispensation, had taken independent stances on macro-economic and other policies, breaching the 'unity' of the alliance on these issues. Invoking Moses Kotane, who is undoubtedly one of the greatest figures in South African revolutionary history and whose contribution spanned decades, is to treat him as representing a particular view of the relationship between ANC and Party. As we have seen, his approach is open to the interpretation that it tended to dissolve the Party as an independent organisation or at least that it was maintained mainly as a symbolic force without establishing its own structures on a formal basis. Obviously that tendency must be read in the context of underground existence and the need to build both ANC and SACP underground organisations, a situation that did not make for purist solutions on questions of Party independence.

There is no doubt that Communists either in the SACP or in the ANC played an important role throughout the history of underground organisation, establishing the initial underground units of the Party and playing a major part in enabling the ANC to survive banning and establish itself underground. Individual Communists were also in the forefront in re-establishing ANC units after Rivonia, sometimes on a very small scale, sometimes on a larger basis. They were also represented in large numbers among those who entered South Africa as MK operatives carrying out daring missions.

Within the overall history of liberation, the Communist underground needs to be seen as opening a new phase, showing that something that had not previously been done could be successfully embarked upon. Continuities and ruptures, it has been noted, mark the history of the national liberation movement. When the Indian Passive Resistance campaign was undertaken in 1946, it impressed Sisulu and Mandela. People were prepared to go to jail, a fate that, Mandela said, still carried a stigma for many Africans.[64] Mandela and Sisulu saw the Defiance Campaign as representing a break with that past.[65]

Likewise, the Communist Party establishment of an underground presence represented a new phase. It showed that illegality did not preclude organisation and the creation of structures. The Party showed it could be done. Even when these units were later crushed, steps were later taken to re-establish organisation under new conditions, carrying out a variety of functions during the entire period of apartheid. For people suffering oppression with apparently no respite, to read or hear of what underground operatives were doing was a source of inspiration and courage. If some could do it, others felt they could too. Without doubt, the experience of the Communists in blazing this trail made it easier for the ANC to follow.

4

THE ANC UNDERGROUND
BETWEEN RIVONIA AND 1976

The accepted view of black, and especially African, politics after the Rivonia Trial, held by historians and other scholars of South African resistance, is conveyed with only limited qualification by Leonard Thompson when he wrote that by the end of 1964 'the first phase of violent resistance was over, and for another decade the country was quiescent.'[1] Another historian commented in similar vein that 'for at least a decade after 1964 the ANC virtually ceased to exist in South Africa and the prospects for liberation appeared more remote than ever.'[2] The same perspective is found in a work published late in 2007.[3] This chapter contests this characterisation. Using evidence from oral interviews and written sources, a picture of a small but significant and growing underground ANC presence in various parts of the country during these years is revealed. It is in fact this very presence that is an important part of the explanation of the subsequent re-emergence of ANC symbols and organisations supportive of the Congress movement, and in particular why it was that the ANC became the primary beneficiary of the Soweto uprising of 1976–7.

Before marshalling the evidence to contradict the notions of dormancy, quiescence, silence and political vacuum, some general observations need to be made about the literature covering this period. It is true that the Rivonia arrests were a 'major breakthrough' for the police, who now 'gained the upper hand in the contest'.[4] As Stephen Davis has written, a 'titanic leap of faith would have been required in 1963 to believe in the ultimate resurrection of the ANC'.[5] But it is not true that the reverses suffered after Rivonia meant that the ANC disappeared altogether, as almost all the literature so confidently asserts.

Part of the reason why people came to believe the ANC had been annihilated was the power and reach of the state, which exerted every effort to ensure that people believed the ANC was dead. Not only was newspaper coverage of the ANC in this period minuscule – which may be accounted for in part by restrictive legislation – but what coverage did occur was extremely negative or dismissive in tone, reflecting the bias of the white-owned newspapers. As for the existence of the ANC outside the country, this was not dealt with in the media, except in order to imply squandering of funds or idle feuding. The Wankie campaign of 1967, for example, received little mention except to refer to MK's failure. It might have raised spirits among ANC supporters at home to know that MK and ZAPU (the Zimbabwe African People's Union), then in alliance with the ANC, inflicted heavy losses on the Rhodesians, as was later conceded by Major-General Ron Reid-Daly[6] of the Selous Scouts, the Rhodesian commandos deployed against guerrillas.

To the extent that the ANC was building an underground presence within the country, its existence depended on highly secretive and unobtrusive organisational activities. The stakes were very high; the odds were stacked against such efforts. Any publicity would have doomed these attempts. Moreover, in a phase where rebuilding or reconstruction is taking place on a new basis, these efforts usually do not show immediate or visible results for some time. In this sense the conditions of underground operations in general have come – at the level of appearances or visibility – to lend support to the view of the ANC's absence.

Before operatives could begin to work, having made an often difficult entry into the country if coming from outside, they needed to 'lie low' and establish that their presence had not been detected. This might mean waiting for some months before even starting with reconnaissance or acquiring material for pamphlets or whatever was required. There were a variety of logistical necessities that were more or less time-consuming, depending on the extent to which a support network was present and had been prepared in advance for the cadre's entry. In the early years, many MK fighters had to fend for themselves and were not met by an internally prepared underground apparatus or any form of logistical support. Linus Dlamini, who was trained primarily in intelligence, entered South Africa without papers and travelled as a stowaway for 11 days on a ship, not eating for the whole journey from Dar es Salaam to Durban. Amos Lengisi and Matthews Ngcobo, also highly trained, spent a longer time in similar conditions leaving Mombasa and entering Cape Town, also without papers, in 1966.[7]

Thus, while little armed activity took place immediately following 1964 and only sporadically during the period thereafter, this is of the nature of underground preparatory work, which, whatever its immediate scale, requires patient rebuilding and is by definition beyond the public eye. Furthermore, the absence of underground structures able to support MK adequately is not the same as the absence of an underground at all. In fact, an underground presence could be quite unrelated to military activities or insufficient to give the full level of support required to mount and sustain an MK presence. Alternatively, it may have been largely geared to sending people out to MK rather than having a capacity to sustain MK cadres on their return from training.[8] Every revolutionary struggle passes through setbacks or changes in emphasis, as in China when there was a change from a worker-led to peasant-driven revolution. These disruptions do not necessarily mean that nothing is happening in the periods before the results of new factors become evident at an overt level.

Here it will be shown that there was a force being trained for underground activity outside the country which, however high its level of training might have been, was not able to be deployed for much of the period of exile. At the same time, people within the country, from very quiet beginnings, gradually developed a 'sea' within which the MK guerrillas could more easily swim as well as independently initiating their own activities – armed and unarmed – that made life difficult for the regime.

A second point is that although the national leadership of the ANC had been arrested in 1964 or gone into exile, the ANC's support base did not simply disappear too.[9] What needs to be recognised is that popular association with the ANC was more than a formal political organisation; it was a cultural link for many people, a connection passed down from many parents to children in a variety of ways, or part of a cultural environment where values were transmitted through various means. Nomboniso Gasa supports this impression from personal experience in the rural Eastern Cape in the 1970s:

Every day, in our families and households, people undermined the state, even as they feared it. Even when there was no mass struggle, there was song and mothers crooned and sang to their children. They whispered the names of Nelson Mandela, Govan Mbeki and Walter Sisulu, Robert Sobukwe, Lilian Ngoyi and Albertina Sisulu in their prayers behind closed doors. Much of this consciousness remained with the supporters of the 'absent' liberation movements.[10]

Then again, people often continued to meet as ANC supporters, though they did little more than exchange views and interpretations, 'spread the word' and keep up one another's spirits. Such was the case in the 1970s (and later) in Ntshingeni, a dusty village adjoining St Mark's mission in Cofimvaba in the Eastern Cape.[11] Many of these people were not ANC members in the technical sense of having 'signed up' – but that is of little significance where the conditions for joining were absent. In some cases, individuals without membership cards did everything else that a 'properly' recruited member would have undertaken in a formally mandated and constituted underground unit. The notion of underground work needs to include a variety of manifestations, including a great deal of freelance supportive activity, such as spontaneous responses to requests to hide people or provide other forms of assistance.[12]

The later reappearance of Congress symbols and activity represented both continuity (for the organisation was never entirely absent) and discontinuity, in that it also undoubtedly spread among people and to areas that may not previously have supported the ANC. Failure to note the element of continuity may relate to a tendency among scholars to focus on what is visible in institutional structures, and hence fail to interrogate absence and silence, to dig below the surface, even a surface calm, to see how and where the 'invisible' associations and formal and informal organisations and other ANC-supporting networks were located.[13]

Though it is not easy to reconstruct the emergence of the ANC underground after 1964, there is sufficient evidence to begin to assemble a picture which by its nature lacks the coherence and complex institutional character of conventional politics. This was a presence which sometimes suffered serious losses, often had to change modes of location, sometimes worked in isolation from other individuals who were not known to one another but were doing similar work. This was part of the post-banning disarray where there was not a centralised coordinating authority and where regularised contact with the ANC's outside mission had not yet been established.

Significantly, many of those involved were women, especially the wives of those in detention, notably Albertina Sisulu, whose role throughout the period of illegality was fundamental to the continued existence of the 'Congress tradition' and presence. These women organised safe accommodation for individuals on the run from the police, and storage facilities for propaganda and publicity equipment. They managed an elaborate communications system and courier network linking the different units. At the same time they ensured that they knew the conditions of various people in need of assistance after experiencing repression and attended to their welfare. There was also a continued role played for those who remained at large, after the arrest of the second High Command.[14]

Albertina Sisulu sought out other ANC figures in an effort to rebuild the organisation. Underground work required a balance between apparent low-profile inactivity (for purposes of police attention) and simultaneously undertaking – under the noses of the police – the difficult task of gradually building 'some semblance of ANC underground machinery.'[15] John Nkadimeng, a stalwart originating from the militant Communist-initiated Northern Transvaal migrant workers' organisation known as Sebatakgomo, and later General Secretary of SACTU, was released from prison in 1966 and then placed under restrictions confining him to Orlando. Security police watched former political prisoners especially closely, so Nkadimeng was slow to make contact with Albertina Sisulu although he had established that she was one of the few ANC figures still active. While it was difficult for her to meet with people like Nkadimeng because of his banning orders and her house arrest, they developed ways of working together while resisting suggestions to engage with what they considered risky participants. Their main activity was to facilitate the passage of ANC members who wanted to leave the country for education or military training. Sisulu and Nkadimeng made contact with Martin Ramokgadi (also a former political prisoner) and indirectly with Robert Manci (known as 'Malume', meaning 'uncle').[16] Together they developed a formal working committee that managed to operate, albeit with difficulty, in order to link with structures in other provinces. This was a problem because the Johannesburg group was not able to meet formally with each other or even communicate at all because of the character of some of the banning orders.[17]

From the outset of this period, in the expectation that individuals were required to leave the country and return as trained soldiers, a priority became recruitment for MK. Some people were unhappy about large numbers leaving the country, but the leadership felt that conditions inside necessitated military preparations outside.[18] Thus, in October 1964, Albertina Sisulu was probably involved in arranging for people from Soweto to leave South Africa for military training and for those returning to instruct others inside the country.[19]

By late 1964 the earliest groups, who had been sent out at the time of the formation of MK, were beginning to return, five of the groups being sent back separately into the country. They were tasked with training others. They were linked to the second High Command, the group led by Wilton Mkwayi, who had evaded arrest at Rivonia and stood trial in what was known as the 'second Rivonia Trial', but they were not directly implicated when Mkwayi and others were charged and continued their work after their arrest. Others were taken out of the country by this group in order to receive training.[20]

The early phase immediately after Rivonia was thus one of patching together what could be joined, and reconnecting with old comrades who were not too afraid to engage in illegal work, especially drawing on the veterans who remained outside prison or prisoners released after relatively short sentences.

While Albertina Sisulu and Nkadimeng were establishing a cell with reach beyond Soweto, another cell organised by Winnie Mandela (now Madikizela-Mandela) was in operation. Albertina Sisulu and also Lilian Ngoyi were reluctant to link up with Winnie Mandela, whose style of operation was considered risky and likely to attract the attention of police agents.[21] Nevertheless, many of those involved in the Winnie Mandela unit were well-established ANC figures like Elliot Tshabangu, Samson Ndou, Rita and Lawrence Ndzanga (Lawrence was later killed in police detention) and it also drew in young people like Wally Serote and Snuki Zikalala.[22] Ndou remarks that underground work never ceased, there was no 'lull', just that general meetings were stopped.[23] The group conducted extensive political education among the younger members on a wide range of aspects of ANC history and Marxism. They were organised on the basis of the M-plan to avoid the arrest of one group implicating and leading to the arrest of another. Ndou and others travelled widely, and he administered an oath based on the MK one to those recruited.[24]

In the late 1960s, despite heavy repression by the state, underground work continued. From mid-1965 until the end of 1969, some 831 people were convicted under an assortment of laws including the Suppression of Communism Act, the Unlawful Organisations Act, the Terrorism Act (from 1968), and the General Law Amendment Act.[25] The types of activity for which people were charged included continuing to be a member of the ANC, taking part in organisational activities, holding ANC meetings, contributing to or soliciting funds for the organisation, conspiring to commit sabotage, recruiting for military training, and undergoing military training abroad. The figure of 831 convictions compares with that of 1604 after the 'waves of mass arrests at the height of political activity in 1963 and 1964'.[26] Some of the former may have been the same people who had been previously convicted and faced 'further charges'.[27]

In this period from the early to the late 1960s, the unit involving Albertina Sisulu and John Nkadimeng was involved in sending people out of the country, distributing ANC and SACP leaflets, recruiting people to carry out tasks, and maintaining underground structures. Through the use of couriers, contact was established and maintained with members in Natal, the Free State and the Western Cape. There were ways in which members of the Johannesburg group could meet twice a month in the centre of the city (drawing on connections with security guards there), contact being coordinated by the Soweto cell, which had links with the leadership in exile and received reports about conditions on Robben Island through newly released prisoners. Another key task continued to be assisting the families of political prisoners, particularly with their financial needs.[28]

Outside Johannesburg, an important indication of underground activity in the late 1960s emerged in the 1969 Pietermaritzburg trial of ANC cadres who had entered the country after training abroad, including as stowaways on ships. The indictment was based on the guerrilla mission identifying secluded places where military training could be provided once arms and ammunition had been smuggled into the country.[29] Members of this group, who entered the country in various ways, had travelled to the Transkei, Eastern Cape, Western Cape, Natal, Transvaal and the Free State, and organised in many of these places. In the case of Amos Lengisi, before his arrest he and his team had 'offered basic military training to a number of recruits. Each batch of newly trained cadres was expected to set up their own structures so that they could provide support for returning guerrillas.'[30] Some of those who were in the Pietermaritzburg trial had taken part in the Wankie campaign; the state joined groups with different origins in the same trial.[31]

The degree of preparation for the entry of the Dlamini–Lengisi –Ngcobo mission seems to have varied, with little logistical support in some cases (for example no travel documentation), very difficult modes of entry (in the case of Linus Dlamini, Matthews Ngcobo and Amos Lengisi, they travelled for between 11 and 20 days as stowaways, depending on whether it was between Dar es Salaam and Durban or Mombasa and Cape Town, most of the time spent in a wardrobe).[32]

A significant element in the strengthening of the ANC underground was the infusion of former political prisoners who had served relatively short-term sentences or had been among the first batch imprisoned. Starting in the late 1960s, prisoners released from the Island gradually started to surface in various townships and rural areas, although they were closely watched by the police. In many cases they were given a mandate to join structures or engage in one or other activity upon their release.[33] This was not peculiar to the ANC, but was also found among PAC returned prisoners like Simon Ramogale in the township of Tembisa in the East Rand in the late 1960s.[34]

Henry Makgothi explains that when he left the Island in the 1970s he knew exactly what he had to do and whom he had to link up with.[35] Murphy Morobe confirms this for the 1980s, when he was 'mandated' to join the trade unions.[36] A group of ex-political prisoners, based in Soweto and Alexandra, worked under heavy security in the late 1960s and early 1970s – in particular, Makgothi, Gqabi, Ramokgadi, Manci and Nkadimeng, though their times of operation did not always coincide.[37]

What is interesting about these underground workers is the element of mutual trust, respect and understanding that developed, and continued to develop, among them, first in the 1950s, then in prison, in MK, in the underground, and for some in exile. Some of those in this Johannesburg grouping who have not died of old age or been assassinated are presently working together in a business in Braamfontein, Johannesburg.

The reach of this group extended beyond the African townships. On release from prison in the 1970s, Indres Naidoo, one of the first members of the Indian community to be convicted of MK activities (a group referred to by the Security Police as the 'dynamite coolies'), returned to his family home in Doornfontein. He was contacted by the Johannesburg group and worked in their underground network.[38]

A number of former political prisoners were also active in establishing an ANC presence in Natal, among them Griffiths Mxenge (later murdered by an apartheid death squad, as was his wife, Victoria) and Mandla Judson Khuzwayo. The role of Jacob Zuma on his release from prison seems to have been crucial in building the ANC in Natal. In an interview he speaks about the situation on his release, contesting the claim that there had been a 'lull' in ANC activity.[39]

Pravin Gordhan, a former ANC underground worker from the mid-1970s, now Commissioner of the South African Revenue Services, speaks of the impact of released political prisoners on the thinking and culture of ANC supporters and as role models for young activists in mid-1970s Natal:

> They were bearers of history, bearers of experiences, bearers of anecdotes, bearers of the Congress culture, 'this is how you do things, this is how you say things, this is how you analyse things', they were bearers of inspiration, because you could relate to them as heroes, and there were not many heroes at the time, and each of them had a different quality because they each played a different role.[40]

This quotation captures an important trait constantly heard as the ANC matured and its presence became felt, and especially important for the underground, conveyed by the phrase 'this is how you do things': sustainable work required careful planning and patient building of organisational structures.

In turn, Barney Pityana, now Vice-Chancellor of the University of South Africa, a founding member of the Black Consciousness movement at the time, speaks of the exemplary character and conduct of people like Griffiths Mxenge and Joe Gqabi, while Terrence Tryon, then a young official of SASO (the South African Students' Organisation), the founding BC organisation, speaks of MD Naidoo, also a released political prisoner, teaching him how to operate underground in the early 1970s.[41]

Gradually the ANC in exile sought to build its ideological hegemony and provide guidance to supporters in the country, an important factor in a period when morale was low and the possibility of recovery of ANC strength seemed unlikely. In the absence of easily available ANC literature and free discussion, it became necessary to try to diffuse general communications about the history and policies of the organisation. Consequently, besides the strengthening and mentorship by former political prisoners, a constant and important factor in the ANC presence within the country was the daily broadcasts from Radio Freedom, repeatedly mentioned by informants as one of the ways they were attracted to the ANC. The lineage of these broadcasts can be traced to the earlier one from an illegal radio station within South Africa, 'ANC Radio', made by Walter Sisulu before his arrest and the subsequent Rivonia Trial.[42] On 26 June 1963 Sisulu broadcast this:

Sons and Daughters of Africa:
I speak to you from somewhere in South Africa.
I have not left the country.
I do not plan to leave.

Later, Wilton Mkwayi made a similar clandestine broadcast, after the Rivonia arrests.[43] For over twenty years Radio Freedom, described as the 'Voice of the African National Congress and the People's Army uMkhonto weSizwe', was broadcast from outside the country. It started from Lusaka, Zambia, in 1967, and at its height broadcast daily at staggered times and frequencies from five African countries: Angola, Ethiopia, Madagascar, Tanzania and Zambia. It is not possible to gauge the extent of its listenership but, as resistance intensified, tuning in to these broadcasts became a daily ritual or duty for those who considered themselves part of the struggle. Listening to these programmes was illegal and construed as 'furthering the aims' of a banned organisation, which could have resulted in a prison sentence. It was thus a form of identification with the ANC in situations where people were already members or were sympathisers but had no opportunity to join. That this was recognised by the regime is illustrated by a 1983 South African commando raid which targeted and destroyed the Radio Freedom Madagascar facility, forcing it off the air for a short period of time.[44]

The broadcasts inspired defiance. They always began with a round of shots from AK47 assault rifles and the revolutionary song 'Hamba kahle Mkhonto weSizwe / Go well, Mkhonto weSizwe'. The sound of gunshots potentially and actually used to attack police and other apartheid targets was inspiring to many people and prompted men and women to seek out the ANC.

But the broadcasts also sought to assign concrete tasks – for the youth, women, workers, civic organisations and others, especially in the 8 January message, delivered on the anniversary of the founding of the ANC. It inspired the creation of organisations amongst unorganised or under-organised sectors and in places that had been neglected. It also helped coordinate the strategies of the ANC internally and externally, ensuring that there was 'one line of march' or that members all 'read from the same prayer book'.

In some ways Radio Freedom was able to achieve these tasks more effectively than many other liberation movement media. In a country characterised by high levels of illiteracy, many people relied on the radio for their information. In addition, commentaries were broadcast in most, if not all, the languages of the country, something not achieved in any other medium.

But engagement in revolutionary struggle entailed continually trying to increase the pressure on the 'enemy' through an increasing and preferably ever more imaginative and extensive range of methods. Radio broadcasts were one means by which the ANC carried its message to South Africans. Another was the sporadic distribution of ANC and SACP propaganda, chiefly pamphlets, much of which were prepared by the SACP in its London office. Initially the material was brought into South Africa by couriers, some of whom were non-South Africans recruited from solidarity movements and the British Communist Party. Once the material had been smuggled in (hidden in the false bottoms of suitcases or wrapped within false covers) it was posted or disseminated among the wider community, though it seems likely that it was also supplied to existing underground units.[45]

The distribution of leaflets was also sometimes accompanied by other ways of making the ANC presence felt. In 1967 ANC flags and huge banners proclaiming 'The ANC lives' appeared on buildings in prominent positions in central Johannesburg and Durban. At the same time as they unfurled through a timing device, they released showers of leaflets down on the streets. Sometimes a pamphlet bomb would be used, a time-delay rocket that on explosion released a payload of pamphlets into the air, usually in a busy concourse. The dramatic effect was often accompanied by a tape-recorded ANC message relayed from a hidden place that would be hard for the police to find. The first such broadcast took place on 26 June 1968 in Johannesburg, and was repeated there as well as in Cape Town, Kimberley and Port Elizabeth during 1969 and 1970. The messages were delivered by Robert Resha, then an ANC leader, and freedom songs were played.[46] These dramatic activities were hard for the media to ignore, and so the news spread to those who had neither seen the pamphlets nor heard the broadcasts.

Other methods were adopted with the same objectives.[47] Stickers bearing the name ANC and the slogan 'Inkululeko ngesikathi sethu / Freedom in our lifetime' were attached to lampposts, walls and shop fronts, and painted slogans would appear referring to the ANC being at war with the regime.[48]

Evidence suggests that such propaganda had real impact. The Revd Fumanekile Gqiba describes their impact in Cape Town in 1975 and 1976:

> I remember some of them at Mowbray bus stop. They used to refer to them as 'bucket bombs', pamphlets that were just blown during the pick-up hour, right in the heart of town, in the main streets. They did a good work, I must say it – they really worked. There was also a heavy publicity on it, press and the like, and blacks again discover, look the ANC's alive. And the method which was used was really sophisticated – as a result, it was said these are well-trained people. People said, 'Ah, our boys have come back,' because we were told that there are some people who went outside to train and they'll be back one day.[49]

By the late 1960s and the 1970s, propaganda units began to establish themselves within South Africa, involving greater use of local cadres, mainly recruited while outside the country. As far as can be ascertained, these units dealt almost solely with propaganda distribution, though their reports on the prevailing situation in the country also assisted

ANC intelligence and strategists. The units of the 1970s were generally very small in number; recruitment took place on a very limited basis and expansion was discouraged.[50] Their membership consisted mainly of Communists. These operatives had to avoid attracting attention to themselves by doing anything that would arouse interest in their lives, for example infringement of the Immorality Act, which prohibited sexual relations across the colour line, or contravention of other apartheid laws that might invite police search of one's possessions and discovery of the unit.[51] Underground white operatives were usually instructed to have no contact with black people – this created a sense of frustration which activists in the open, nonracial movement of the 1980s would not experience. If, in the earlier period, an underground operative had entered a township or demonstrated any degree of empathy or solidarity, this would have led to their underground activities being immediately endangered if not ended. For the white operative, being underground entailed living an elaborate double life.[52]

Propaganda units continued to disseminate material that had been smuggled into the country, including SACP or ANC publications like *Sechaba* and the *African Communist*, but they also began to produce material of their own. In many cases the literature was official literature of the ANC or SACP, sent from outside but produced within the country on time-consuming, manually operated duplicators known as 'roneo machines'. Otherwise, pamphlets without the official imprimatur of either organisation but supportive of the broad lines of the ANC–SACP alliance were written and produced by these units. In this category was the publication *Vukani! / Awake!*[53] Then too there was general, anti-apartheid material such as bumper stickers that read 'Ban apartheid, not people.' As Pallo Jordan comments, these were slogans 'anyone could use. It wasn't seen as ANC and anyone could be saying that. But it was injecting a certain mood into the country.'[54]

At the same time, ANC propaganda activity was often spontaneously organised by or included people who were not members of the ANC or SACP. In the years after the ANC's banning there was periodic spray-painting of ANC slogans by informal groups sympathetic to the organisation. The officially constituted propaganda units coexisted with freelance activities of people in support of the ANC and SACP, who sometimes devised their own pamphlets or painted slogans on walls.[55] This tendency towards spontaneous propaganda activity was heightened during and after the Soweto uprising, which was accompanied by 'a spectacular outpouring of agitational leaflets'.[56] The Johannesburg *Star* of 16 October 1976 commented: 'Circulating mainly in Black urban areas and varying widely in quality of writing, production and thinking, their very number sometimes gives the impression that everyone with access to a typewriter and a duplicating machine has rushed to propagate his own views.'

The ANC of the mid-1970s entered a situation where the voice and imagery of the organisation had not been legally available for some fifteen years and where many individuals were ignorant of its existence and policies. The only visible black politicians were those who collaborated with the government in bantustans, urban 'Bantu' councils and similar institutions. Propaganda efforts had the effect of keeping the memory of the ANC alive within the country, maintaining a visibility when it was illegal to be organisationally present.

The ANC was primarily urban-based and that is where it drew most of its MK recruits. Much of what has been described so far took place in the cities and urban centres of the country. But it had made organisational gains in parts of the rural areas at various times. The rural areas included numbers of past and potential supporters; though they were more isolated, dispersed and difficult to access, they were unevenly policed (sometimes with police presence very concerted and sometimes relatively absent) and could conceal ANC activity more easily than people in the towns. In the two examples that follow, one in the then Western Transvaal (now North-West Province) and the other in the Transkei, support for the ANC went hand in hand with opposition to the bantustan structures that the apartheid government sought to impose.

Around the time of the Rivonia Trial the community of Dinokana near Zeerust in the Western Transvaal had just emerged from intense conflict with the government over the Bantu Authorities system, attempts to depose their chief, and later the extension of passes to women, involving an unusual alliance of patriarchs and women.[57] In cases where hereditary chiefs would not cooperate they were replaced by government nominees. One of those who were uncooperative was Chief Moilwa of Dinokana. When instructed to tell his wife to take out a pass he is alleged to have said, 'Who the hell is Verwoerd? He is just a minister and there will be other ministers after him. I am not afraid of him, and Dinokana will stand here forever.'[58] The resistance went further and some of the chiefs decided to throw their weight behind the ANC. They had set up underground structures, which they linked to MK and its recruitment machineries. In a meeting of a village council (*lekgotla*), the views of the chiefs were discussed and it was decided that each family would provide one of its sons to join MK.[59]

This was referred to as the 'decision under the tree', a tree opposite the current offices of the chief's councillors. As with many physical objects around which significant events and rituals occur or to which ritual significance is attached, this tree has peculiar qualities in that, as I have seen, its branches fall off at the slightest touch. I note that I have seen this happen because a reader of an article where this was mentioned suggested insertion of the word 'appear', implying that the phenomenon was an illusion.[60] This transformation of the scale of Dinokana resistance is illustrative of a frequent political phenomenon whereby local grievances if skilfully managed can be transformed into a willingness to commit to wider national issues, in this case providing human resources for MK.

In another remote area, Ntshingeni, a village adjoining St Mark's mission in the district of Cofimvaba, attempts were made to keep the ANC alive during the 1970s and 1980s.

In the 1970s ... I used to meet with [a group of three] people ... about ANC. We used to talk generally about the situation in the country, and then we could say this one is ANC and this one is PAC, after the banning of the organisations ... We usually had *mgalelo* [a type of *stokvel*, an informal savings scheme, found in South Africa]. We used to meet in the *stokvel*, and there we made each other aware that they should not be treated the way they were treated by the Matanzima government. We organised people. We tried not to hit [get caught by] Matanzima's laws. When the organisation was unbanned now, all those people joined the ANC.

Operating in that period required secrecy and that is why they chose to operate in the *stokvels*. They knew that there were informers present. Their tactics were flexible, and included infiltrating bantustan structures:

There were a lot [of informers]. We used to discuss in front of them and they used to nickname us communist and *abanqolobi* [terrorists]. All those names ... We joined a women's organisation in Transkei which was called TUWO, Transkei United Women's Organisation. In the true sense it was TNIP, Matanzima's party. So we decided to join it and sensitise the other women that this is not it, not what has been fought for and people were aware that there were campaigns that Mandela should be released. So everywhere our group went in the Transkei, we wanted to hear people talking about Mandela. If they did not talk about Mandela we knew this was not the organisation we were thinking of. It was generally informal, but we discussed that we should defy Matanzima. We used to say one day the ANC will be unbanned, but there were no people to guide us.[61]

This last statement indicates the dilemma of freelance ANC supporters. They wanted to act in a way that supported the ANC, but not being in touch with leadership or formal structures meant they sometimes had doubts as to whether they were in fact doing what the organisation would have required. They may often have used this freedom in creative ways that the organisation would have admired. Alternatively they could have done things apparently in the name of the ANC that were embarrassing. Logistically the dilemma was impossible to resolve. But somehow, through talk with trusted associates, news spread of how to connect with the ANC where it was present, and there was at times an MK presence and assisting of MK in other parts of the former Transkei, including activity of a member of Matanzima's family:

We also knew that there was somebody from Cradock who was a policeman in Lady Frere who used to help the people who were going out on MK, his name was Zolile Tshonti. He helped them to cross. Zolile was related to the Matanzimas, they never suspected that he was doing this. They only heard about this at his funeral. This man used to stay at Lingelihle Township near Cradock.[62]

The isolation of the rural areas was a severe obstacle to the dissemination of ANC views and activity, but on occasion the apartheid government unwittingly assisted the organisation by banishing troublesome opponents to the bantustans or former political prisoners to the rural areas from which they had originally come. The influence of people banished under apartheid legislation was important in spreading the message of the ANC, establishing structures and initiating activities.[63] They helped to mentor potential leaders, inspire new recruits, and sustain the spirit of opposition within the local communities where they settled. A number of examples must suffice here.

A former ANC leader, Dr James Njongwe, was banished to Matatiele in the Transkei. Here he helped set up ANC networks that were linked to his sons, in particular Boy Njongwe. One of those who came into the orbit of Boy Njongwe was Nompumelelo Setsubi.[64] Nompumelelo Setsubi started to draw close to ANC thinking as a Fort Hare student in the early 1970s, listening to Radio Freedom together with a group of trusted friends. When she became a teacher in Matatiele, Boy Njongwe recruited her to the ANC. The process of induction entailed carefully discussing her understanding of politics, and upon recruitment he took her through a process of thorough political education. She then performed various underground tasks, mainly related to the production of ANC propaganda. While some of this literature was introduced from outside the country, it was often translated into Xhosa and Sotho (Matatiele being near to Lesotho and containing a majority Sotho-speaking population). Njongwe encouraged Setsubi to analyse the issues of the day and to write and produce pamphlets with a local content, speaking to questions immediately affecting people in the area.[65] The level of secrecy and sophistication involved in this network is reflected in Setsubi's husband also being an underground operative, but the two of them never speaking about it to each other until much later.

A second example comes from Heilbron in the Free State. Here Mongezi Radebe, an activist who grew up in the village, also recalls the influence of people who were banished:

> In our township we had a granny called Ma Mokhele who used to tell us a lot about black history. Later I started understanding that she had been a member of the ANC and she had been sent to Heilbron under banishment. So she used to explain a lot of these things: what they were doing in the Women's League, what ANC was in the initial stages when it became militant, when the young ones like Mandela came into it. She was explaining its historical significance and why we should be proud

of it, and why we should take on from where they've left. And that's how we started understanding a lot of things politically.

Radebe also developed politically through reading, including banned literature, which he claimed was not uncommon to find on some farms.[66]

A third example comes from the Northern Transvaal. A veteran Robben Islander, Peter Nchabaleng, who was later murdered in police custody, organised ANC supporters in Sekhukhuneland. Nchabaleng maintained contact with Ramokgadi, one of the former political prisoners who built the underground together with Albertina Sisulu and others, who brought Tokyo Sexwale, a trained MK soldier and later a prominent politician, with him. During his visit to the area, Sexwale provided political education as well as military training.[67]

Confirmation of extensive ANC underground networks in the rural towns and villages of the former Transkei – in the period of 'quiescence'– is also provided from a quite different source, a confidential interview with a former Transkeian security policeman. He indicated the continued existence of underground networks after Rivonia, often around former political prisoners or other banished individuals but also established on other bases throughout the post-Rivonia period. He referred particularly to people released from prison and being banished to the area and then leaving the country. There were also others who, the police discovered, had been in exile and were infiltrating after having undergone military training.[68]

◎

The years in which the ANC attempted to establish its underground presence saw the emergence and growth above ground of the Black Consciousness movement (BCM) in the country, especially among young intellectuals and university students. In time the new movement, given the illegality of a public ANC presence, appeared to challenge the ANC's hegemony within the anti-apartheid struggle. Although it gradually experienced increased state repression, the BCM was not banned until 1977, and initially at least it enjoyed considerable space to propagate its views. This freedom was allowed partly because the apartheid regime at first perceived the BCM's emphasis on blackness as a vindication of its policy of 'separate development'.[69]

Some BC leaders dismissed the ANC and PAC and regarded themselves as the vanguard of the struggle or were ignorant of the history of the struggle or the continued existence of the ANC. Some of those then involved in BC were very clear that this was a trend that was not shared by the general membership.[70] Others like Barney Pityana depict this as a later phenomenon, resulting partly from the restrictions placed on many of the original leadership and their positions being taken by less experienced individuals.[71]

Then, too, many of the young generation of BC activists were contemptuous of the slow efforts at rebuilding ANC structures, in so far as they were aware of them. Lindiwe Sisulu, when attracted to BC, · knew of her mother's activity in the ANC underground:

> Lindi meanwhile knew that her mother was politically active but did not think much about what she was doing: 'I felt that mama, [John] Nkadimeng and company were just concerned with setting up structures. They were not involved in any action. Their lack of activity confirmed my idea of a dead organisation.'[72]

Nkosazana Dlamini (now Dlamini-Zuma), when joining the ANC from the BC camp around the time of the Soweto uprising, still thought of the ANC as moving too slowly:

> When I say we wanted to meet the ANC, we wanted to join the ANC, it does not mean that we didn't have any reservations – we did think they were a bit slow. Even after having spoken to them and appreciating the problems they were facing, we still felt that. But we felt that to make them fast we had to actually help them: join the ANC and try and put our enthusiasm into the ANC.[73]

On its side, some figures in the ANC were critical of the rise of Black Consciousness. It was considered short-sighted and based narrowly on 'race'. Instead of concentrating on ensuring its survival in the long term by building solid organisational capacity, the BCM in this view relied on consciousness-raising and the power of ideology: 'all talk and no action'.

At the same time, there were figures in both camps who saw the two trends operating without competition and rivalry. A founder and leading figure of the BCM, Barney Pityana, who came from an ANC family background, kept in regular contact with ANC figures and never saw the BCM as supplanting the ANC. Other evidence exists from the 1970s that the ANC presence was recognised by BC adherents and that ANC literature was read widely in these circles.[74] Papi Mokoena, a SASO activist expelled from Fort Hare University in 1973, recalls:

> I think contact with the ANC was growing. More people from outside were coming into the country, books were coming from outside. There was a dearth of material at that time: published material of the ANC was particularly valuable and one treasured it as if it was gold. We even had a 'mobile library' – books which moved from hand to hand amongst selected people. You see, we knew the ANC was underground, but the problem was finding the underground members of the ANC. At that time more and more of them were coming out of prison and coming to see us, SASO, to see who we were. We used to listen to Radio Freedom every day when there was broadcast. We were not anti ANC's political ideas at that time – never – because we felt that it is a liberation movement, we are a students' movement and these are the people we need, we want to have the material they are giving us. That is why SASO became so receptive to ANC ideas later on. The situation was constantly developing; we were meeting hard practice which could not be fitted onto those ideas which we had developed in college.[75]

The more farsighted and less sectarian ANC figures appreciated that BC had injected something new and positive into the South African political scene, opening spaces that had been closed, helping to reassert black dignity and pride, and producing a spirit of resistance and unity between all sections of the black population. Whatever reservations may have been felt, these did not detract from the positive factors. This was the position of Walter Sisulu when visited by his son Lungi, who shared the feeling in sections of the ANC underground that there was a danger that the BCM might try to position itself as a replacement of the ANC. This anxiety was further fuelled by the attitude in some BC circles that the ANC was a conservative and apathetic organisation whose nonracial politics were inimical to the liberation of black people. Walter Sisulu, however, explained, 'We in the ANC did not regard the emergence of the Black Consciousness movement as hostile. We regarded it as part and parcel of the struggle and we welcomed it as a progressive idea.'[76]

A similar willingness to engage with the BCM guided most of the Robben Islanders and ex-Robben Islanders.[77] Outside prison, people like Jacob Zuma, Joe Gqabi, Albertina Sisulu and others entered into relationships with BC people that were neither disrespectful nor patronising, although they did feel that BC had serious limitations. Barney Pityana speaks warmly of the response received from Winnie Mandela who, he said, never made any attempt to draw BC people into ANC structures.[78]

The engagement of ANC underground members with BC was obviously meant to win BC supporters over to the ANC. To what extent this also entailed appreciation of the importance of the BCM is not clear. But the generally respectful relationship was probably an important factor in the gradual winning over of many BC people before and after 1976.[79] Much of this happened through individual mentoring, as the example of Joe Gqabi reveals. Gqabi, a leading ANC figure, later assassinated in Zimbabwe, was released from prison in the early 1970s and played an important role in influencing BC activities in the Transvaal as well as building the ANC underground. Nat Serache, then a journalist on the *Rand Daily Mail*, offers an insight into Gqabi's role. On going to interview him for the newspaper, Serache says Gqabi turned the interview into 'political education' and introduced him to the ANC. From that day onwards 'I worked with him very secretly.' Serache was then involved in BC structures, though these were loosely defined at the time. Although he was ready to abandon these and concentrate on the ANC, Gqabi encouraged him to remain within BC and to influence its direction. In fact Gqabi was indirectly to influence some developments during the 1976 uprising.[80] At a meeting attended by Serache with BC comrades it was decided to 'go and close down all the shebeens [formerly illicit liquor outlets and favoured social haunts of many Africans in South Africa] in Soweto because they were distracting people from taking part in the struggle.' Serache reported this to Gqabi:

> He said, 'Ja, it is true liquor is destroying our people, but I wonder whether if we go and close the shebeens the way you are preparing to do we would not be driving both the patrons and the shebeen owners to the side of the enemy? Because what will happen if the police see

this as the opportunity to come and defend the shebeen owners? Are we not going to become the enemy?' he asked, and this immediately opened my eyes. He said: 'Obviously we need these people, they are our people. We want to involve them in the struggle but is this the right way of doing things because once the police come and protect them we become the enemy and the police become their friends?'

Serache returned to his BC comrades and presented Gqabi's arguments as his own, and they accepted his view that the proposal was counterproductive. Serache says Gqabi did not have any direct contact with BC people but continued to advise indirectly.[81] He also pursued a process of continued political and security training with Serache.

Another example of a personal dynamic in the relationship between ANC and BC is provided by the Sisulu family:

Despite Albertina [Sisulu]'s concerns about the BCM, she was supportive of [her daughter] Lindi's involvement. Lindi appreciated the fact that her mother did not patronise her during their political discussions: 'She did not say her way was better. She took all the time to discuss and explain. She had more time for me than ever before. In a way I was her conduit for what was happening out there. She was not hostile to Black Consciousness, but she was aware of its limitations and she associated it with the radicalism of the youth.'[82]

Albertina Sisulu later played a similar, albeit more active, role in the political transformation of the thinking of her son Zwelakhe, then a leading journalist:

I had to educate Zwelakhe back from BC. He had been influenced by his journalist friends.[83] I had to sit him down at the kitchen table and teach him about history and about his family. [I explained that] not every white is responsible for repression, but just a few. Whites were born here and have a right to be here; many have no other place to go ... I sent him home with some books ... and when he came back, he said, 'Mom, you were right.'[84]

The relationship between the two organisations was thus much more fluid and coextensive than is generally allowed. Not only did many

BC people simultaneously interact with the ANC, admire the ANC or belong to ANC structures underground, but the very direction of the BCM was itself open to debate and discussion within the movement.

Masterpiece Gumede, who joined SASO at the University of Zululand in 1972, recalls that 'in terms of rhetoric, I think we were close to the PAC, but the people we wanted to be with were people like Mandela and Luthuli and ANC people'.[85] Ralph Mgijima indicates widespread overlap between the ANC underground and BC in the student community on the University of Natal (black) campus, which enjoyed a relatively liberal environment.[86] Consequently, it was easier in such a situation to blur differences between the legal BC and the illegal ANC. But this overlap appears, from interviews already cited, to have extended well beyond this institution.

One of the weaknesses of scholarship in many areas of the humanities is that it tends to work with dichotomies, so that one is forced to choose between binary opposites. It is either this or it is that. That is not how the real world works, but in a dichotomous spirit there has been a tendency to assume a consistent and universally antagonistic, oppositional or competitive relationship between ANC and BC, and that individuals must have chosen one or the other. While this chapter provides a mere glimpse into the connections and interactions, it does indicate that relationships varied and were extremely complex and can in no sense be reduced to an oppositional, or obviously irreversible, tendency towards BC absorption within the ANC. The BCM was an autonomous movement and some of its distinct influences remain within the ANC today. At the same time, the ANC had sufficient depth, derived from its decades of experience, generally to be able to listen and learn and interact in a manner that drew BC closer and made the relationship more constructive and cooperative over the years that followed.

◎

The blanket description of black politics after Rivonia as one of 'silence' and 'absence' has held sway in the literature till now. It may often have been silent for reasons of security in the initial establishment of illegal underground units, but absence is a quite different matter. Two historiographical consequences have flowed from this. One has led to the unproblematised explanation of the 1976 Soweto uprising as simply being directed by BC forces, with the ANC entirely absent.[87] This chapter has not sought to argue that the ANC initiated that uprising but to show that the ANC was 'there' and at times played some role in its unfolding and direction. It also played a substantial part when activists (including those not aligned to the ANC) were in danger and sought to escape into exile.[88] It was there in its own right, but also as a presence within the BC movement.

The prevailing notion of 'absence' has also left unexplained the re-emergence of Congress symbols and organisations in the late 1970s and 1980s. Why did Congress organisations, and not BC, derive this benefit? This cannot be explained without understanding the presence of the ANC throughout the post-Rivonia period and the character of its organisational input as one of the key factors leading to later 'Congress hegemony'. The reason why the ANC had a better chance of survival than BC was its emphasis on building structures.

This inability to understand what was really happening on the ground, or rather underground, derives from the ANC being more than an organisation for many people. Even after banning, it remained a cultural presence in many houses, drawn on in conversations and as a reference point. Sometimes it was used to warn young people of what might happen if they followed Mandela's route.[89] Even this negative allusion was an indication of the presence of the ANC in people's consciousness.[90] But this cultural character, this tradition of allegiance, was also a reservoir of support for the organisation. People continued to regard themselves as ANC where they had been that before, though obviously many did waver. Thousands of people who had been members had not been jailed or exiled. The thousands who had never joined but supported the organisation may sometimes have been cowed by the might of the apartheid state.[91] But the 'Congress consciousness' did not simply disappear, even if people may have been cautious and wary, and carefully sounded others out before indicating their sympathies.

Repression did lead some people into collaboration or to join alternative organisations, though this was not always unambiguous, with apparent collaborators actually assisting underground operatives in some cases.[92] It may also have signalled, in many cases, a change of convictions and loyalties. But repression does not guarantee a shift in convictions or removal of the potential to act on these. The capacity to oppress and repress does not provide any 'home' in itself, nor guarantee that people shift their loyalty to the government or structures it sets up.

The underground organisation was the vehicle for drawing these sympathies into organised form, on a basis that made some contribution towards the development of the 1976 uprising, and in fact it was in dialogue with BC organisations from their earliest days. The underground was also the organised force that provided access to an enduring political home with the capacity to channel those who wanted to leave BC into a movement that had an organisationally sustainable basis. This relates both to the ANC underground and to the capacity which it displayed to absorb the large numbers of youth that crossed the borders. Because of disarray and division, expulsions and counter-expulsions, among other factors, the PAC proved relatively disabled. It is a paradox that the undoubted body of support that PAC enjoyed at its inception and through continued responses to the Africanist message never managed to be turned into a wide-scale and sustained organisational presence.

In the end it was the slow and patient reinsertion of the ANC into the country, taking advantage of the loyalty and sympathy of veteran members, that ensured that when the time came, the ANC would emerge as the pre-eminent anti-apartheid force in the process leading to establishing a democratic order.

5

THE CHARACTER OF
UNDERGROUND WORK

Till now there has been no attempt to characterise the ANC underground in South Africa as an experience with specific political, sociological, psychological and other implications. By its nature, organisation and political activity underground are very different from other ways of practising politics. In addition, the South African situation introduced conditions that were unique and that raised fairly distinct issues and problems. This chapter is a first venture at outlining the practical, social and moral qualities and tendencies that characterised modes of organising the ANC underground in the period up to 1976. It is based on insights from my own experience as a one-time underground operative, as well as on data from interviews conducted with a fairly wide range of underground participants active from the 1950s onwards.

Underground work is a form of political activism requiring certain tools necessary to safeguard secrecy as well as calling for a personal commitment that will sustain people through adverse conditions. Most people who entered underground units knew they faced great dangers. They only needed a sprinkling of knowledge of resistance history to appreciate that, from the earliest days after the ANC's banning and especially after the introduction of detention without trial, people were routinely tortured and sometimes killed. The prospect of a similar fate ensured that many or possibly most underground cadres possessed a high degree of moral commitment. Moreover, as operatives worked often under very difficult conditions, their survival generally required considerable understanding of the reasons for their sacrifice and a degree of political maturity.

Underground activity, as an experience, involves distinct styles of work that are quite different from open political activity. Few of the qualities that distinguish conventional democratic politics can be found in underground organisation. It must, by definition, lack a public element, just as it generally lacks features considered essential to democratic debate and consultation. It happens in the shadows, out of sight. By virtue of its seclusion, it provides opportunities for performing worthy activities as well as abuse. But, as with other moments of ANC-SACP history, there are no Chinese walls between above-ground and underground phases or the experiences and identities associated with them. Many individuals have been involved in both legal and illegal activities at different times or simultaneously, and have taken habits from one mode of organisation into the other. Indeed, some of these ways of working may still have a bearing on the way certain activists or leaders operate today.

Successful underground activity requires intense secrecy, even or especially at the personal and interpersonal levels. People who are underground generally cannot 'open their hearts' to their lovers or anyone else if they want to ensure their own survival and protect those they love. Many of the values that one might conventionally expect in a range of relationships tend to be negated. Underground work often makes it impossible to 'service' them in the usual way, because of the dangerous conditions under which tasks are done. What is normally a source of comfort or solace may become a danger or a potential basis for suspicion. A veteran from the 1940s, John Nkadimeng, expressed the dilemma in the advice he used to give MK cadres infiltrating South Africa.

> You see, these boys used to come to me when they were coming back into the country and I would give them instructions, and ... say to them: 'You know who is your enemy now? For you to succeed in your ... [operation] it is your mother [who is the danger]. Never go to your mother. If you do go to your mother you are finished. Because your mother will be so excited she is going to tell her cousin, her friend, and then it will be known that you are here and the enemy is sitting there and waiting for this type of information. So you can't succeed. Your mother, your sister, your girlfriend, your good friend, not one of them.[1]

In fact, the police were prepared for lapses arising from any manifestations of 'normality' such as the resumption of ordinary relationships that had existed before people joined MK. They would watch the houses of relatives closely in case MK operatives visited, and this is confirmed by the Security Police.[2] Linus Dlamini, who infiltrated the country after stowing away on a ship from Dar es Salaam, was forced to seek refuge with his brother; although he moved from place to place, it was by following his brother that the police were led to him.[3]

The need to stay away from those with whom operatives had close bonds became all the more imperative once the ANC's social base had been disrupted after Rivonia. Ideally some form of reliance on family and friends should have been a natural resource in underground situations. But with the disruption that occurred at Rivonia, this could not be so.

Yet the advice of Nkadimeng would not always be applicable. It depended on individual circumstances and the changing conditions of underground work over time. As the struggle intensified, the ways operatives were deployed varied considerably and required different ways of surviving to work effectively; new coping styles were needed at times on a case-by-case basis and as the general political situation changed. At the time to which Nkadimeng refers, tens of thousands of young militants had been sent out of the country or chose to leave it, and many of these were known to the police, who watched the homes of their families in the expectation of their return within a certain period. There was a pattern that those who had left established. The large numbers who left at the instance of the liberation movement may have been prompted by the weakness of the underground in the late 1970s and early 1980s. But the effect of this exodus was to disrupt the organic connection between militancy and the natural base of the cadres in their community, family and among the masses. At a later period, as the struggle intensified on a range of fronts, the opposite of what Nkadimeng advised became closer to the norm, with many underground operatives seeking networks of family and friends as their basic source of support.

At the same time, there were cases where the success of underground operations depended on confiding in loved ones or people outside the immediate illegal activity in which they were engaged and obtaining their assistance. This was true for Zubeida Jaffer. Having remained in the country throughout, she was active in the Western and, to a lesser extent, Eastern Cape in the 1970s and 1980s, both publicly and underground. Unlike returning operatives, she depended very much on family and broader community connections. Her work would have been impossible in the conditions of absolute secrecy and relative isolation of most MK missions, especially the earlier ones.[4] In fact this ability to draw on family and friends was also essential to the early organisation of the underground when adequate preparations for the reception of MK operatives could not be made.[5] All the same, the necessity to keep an assignment or presence absolutely secret tended to prevail, given the conditions of underground.

In underground organisation, conspiratorial methods rule. This is partly because the work tends to consist of the activities of small groups of people. The reconstruction of the ANC and SACP underground after Rivonia was designed in small-scale units. People worked on a 'need to know' basis: person X may have interacted with person Y on one activity, but Y ought not to have known that X also related to person Z in connection with other activities.

Within the units the degree of professionalism varied. Professionalism depended largely on the level, character and effectiveness of training. It also related to how closely a unit could maintain its links with its command structures and 'handlers'. Having recourse to the advice of experienced cadres often served as effectively as training courses. It was harder to avoid errors where one operated without others, especially without those more experienced, who might point to potential dangers or indicate defects in planned or ongoing activities.

Some cadres received years of training of various kinds in many countries; others had a three-week crash course inside or outside the country. Still others were not trained at all, and many acted freelance. The kind of training received determined the type of activities a unit or individual was capable of conducting, how it was planned and executed, and the level of risk involved. If a guerrilla unit operated on a very professional basis, after an attack it would have an escape route and, in case of problems, a fallback escape route. But there would be both commonly agreed fallback positions and escape routes, and individual ones not known to other members of the group. Even in units where there was a high degree of trust and comradeship, chances could not be taken through unnecessary sharing of information.[6]

In general, communication and sharing of information were kept minimal. The joy of achievement was not usually celebrated beyond those who were involved directly in an operation, when they were able to be together afterwards without running any risks. On the other hand, staying together in one place might have been the most secure situation when movement was dangerous or when alternative places of accommodation could not easily be found for the various unit members. Often, the most carefully planned operation was disrupted by the unexpected. That being so, one could not conduct guerrilla operations on rigid guidelines and expectations that everything planned would unfold as envisaged.

Security considerations, surveillance, countersurveillance, and the dangers of infiltration required a degree of single-mindedness and even ruthlessness. This led some units to execute suspected or known informers. There are well-documented cases of execution, as when an MK unit killed Bartholomew Hlapane, who had been a state witness in numerous political trials. Leonard Nkosi, a deserter from the Wankie campaign, who became an *askari* (working for the South African police), was also executed later.[7] Interestingly, the police tended not to trust the *askaris* fully because they had often been recruited after threats of death.[8]

The qualities and requirements which have been suggested as characteristic of underground work ran counter to the normal practices of open, democratic political activity – but of course, they were dictated by unusual circumstances. Nevertheless, their effects could well have continued beyond the period of insurrection and some analysts have claimed that this mindset continues to influence the current practices of ANC leaders and rank-and-file. In particular, critics of the recently defeated ANC President and current State President, Thabo Mbeki, point to the high degree of secrecy and lack of openness that are said to characterise his mode of practising politics as opposed to what is supposed to happen in a public democratic order. This is seen as relating to a legacy of illegal struggle where security was uppermost. Indeed, in so far as the ANC operated within militarised and fairly commandist parameters in exile and underground, it was a condition where a high degree of centralised authority, stability, continuity and homogeneity of values was stressed. This was seen as necessary for survival amid continued attacks and attempted sowing of division, which had led among other things to the assassination of many of the individuals whose contribution is recorded in this book.

In the course of underground operations, certain activities had to be carried out with precision and be correctly timed, with careful reconnaissance and other logistical preparations. Technical proficiency, of varying kinds and levels, was essential to ensure success. But the requirements of technical proficiency and careful observation of the 'rules' could at times lead to a degree of depoliticisation,[9] to political blind spots, just as some intensely theoretical people or those who spent a great deal of time on their own political development, for example reading and developing theoretical understanding, were sometimes insufficiently skilled in technical matters and, in having to perform them, might have created dangers. The people who were inclined to read books and write pamphlets, like those who were not so attuned to intellectual work but knew all about explosives and detonating various devices, created their own potential dangers or limitations.

Where the qualities were combined in the individuals composing a unit the dangers were lessened, but where an individual operated alone there could be more risk. Where people were preoccupied with the technical side of getting things done, lack of political engagement could lead to demoralisation or lack of focus on the long term. Those producing and issuing pamphlets on a large scale, for example, had to concentrate on various practical tasks – duplicating, buying stationery, distribution and so on. It is important to appreciate today that right up until the late 1970s there were few, if any, accessible and secure photocopying machines and that duplication was a time-consuming and messy activity usually involving a hand-operated machine.[10] And if pamphlets were distributed by a 'bucket bomb' set off with a timing device, usually attached to a tape-recorded message, there were additional technical requirements that were far more complicated than simply posting.

Even for a simple propagandist using a post box, the envelopes could not all be dumped in one box because that would make interception easy. The operative would need a mental picture of the location of very many post boxes throughout the area of operation. Envelopes had to be of a variable type and size, and the way addresses were written or typed could not be uniform. Such precautions made interception more difficult. All these activities are mundane – but expertise here could make the difference between reaching thousands and reaching only ten people or none. This illustrates one of the essential features of underground work, that many of the precautions needed were more or less common sense or what could be learnt in a detective novel. But these simple precautions needed to be observed for success or to avoid arrest.

If one was not composing the pamphlets oneself and was responsible purely for distribution, the political element was separate from that task. The political quality of the action was initiated by others. Although the action was political in its effect, the operative's practical activity itself was not; and unless the operative was part of a unit that conducted discussions or political education among its members, there was a real danger of alienation from the political character of the activity and its result.

The process of recruitment and deployment generally did not provide the opportunity for monitoring operatives on a personal level. What is more, people also changed over time and in response to what they experienced; many suffered psychological difficulties, sometimes unbeknown to those in charge. It was not unknown for underground operatives trained outside the country to find conditions so difficult at a personal and psychological level that they abandoned the work and returned overseas.[11] A psychological problem may have been lurking or emerged unobserved, only to have decisive effect in moments of inactivity or stress (perhaps in danger or after arrest). This issue of stress was especially important where persons were recruited for intelligence-gathering, when state institutions were infiltrated. Providing information sometimes put inordinate strain on the person supplying the data.

Similarly, in sabotage or combat operations involving a wide range of technical activities, some of the elements of potential depoliticisation were present, others absent. In sabotage it is often easier to see the reaction to what has been done. Eric Mtshali describes the pleasure of hearing people in a taxi discussing one of the successes of his unit.[12] Clearly, if an operative was near a place where a bomb was set off, reaction could be heard or more easily established. The first phase of success was simply to know that it had 'gone off'. But often the saboteur had to get far away in order to ensure safety and avoid capture. One must understand the psychological importance of knowing that what had been done at considerable risk had actually succeeded. Underground work was lonely. People were not part of a sports team, who would congratulate one another, or whose fans would applaud. It should be recalled that the media seldom reported on underground activities, especially propaganda work. Consequently, there was a sense of emptiness that an operative felt until knowing that the operation had achieved some measure of success in reaching its target.

As with other forms of underground work, the extent to which cadres exhibited a depoliticised technicism may have depended on how they worked, whether alone or in a unit, and what opportunities existed for meeting and holding political discussion. It is clear that thoroughgoing processes of induction were often implemented.[13] This is especially true if we treat underground activity as starting from the moment the operation was prepared, in camps and other political schools outside the country, where intensive and extensive processes of political training and discussion occurred,[14] even if considerable time had to elapse between preparing and doing the job.

It was also difficult to sustain political discussion as a living and continuous part of the unit's activity when inside the country. Given that every meeting held some point of danger, unit members tended to be isolated from one another when contact was not needed for operational activities. Isolation obviously enhanced the possibility of depoliticisation. On the other hand, people had to meet together to identify and discuss targets unless these had been selected beforehand from 'outside'. And the choice of MK targets generally reflected political assessments. For example, the attack on a police station in Soekmekaar in the current Limpopo Province (formerly the far northern part of the Transvaal) was based on the unit's understanding of community anger at police involvement in forced removals.[15] Likewise, the attacks in 1977–80 on the Moroka and Orlando police stations in Soweto and the one in Booysens were aimed at organs of state power identified in the minds of ordinary people with intense repression.[16]

An elitist element is characteristic of underground activity. This was implicit in the early Communist conceptions of a vanguard party. In his 1902 work, *What Is to be Done?*, Lenin premised his notion of a vanguard on the need for theory to be brought to the working class from outside, by intellectuals.[17] Without this external influence, he claimed, the working class was condemned to the spontaneous, to trade union as opposed to revolutionary consciousness. Even before Lenin, Plekhanov, regarded as the founder of Russian Marxism, had advanced these ideas in more extreme form, seeing the intelligentsia standing almost '*in loco parentis* over the infant workers' movement.'[18]

This idea of bringing ideas to the working class 'from outside' is found from an early stage in CPSA statements. In 1921 a South African delegation report to the Comintern, referring to Africans, noted, 'This primitive mass is waiting to be stirred.'[19] Even fifty years later, SACP pamphlets issued with such titles as *Vukani! / Awake!* implied that the masses had to be disturbed from their slumbers by those who were more advanced.[20] Although the subjective state of mind of those initiating political activities of various kinds was not necessarily elitist, their pronouncements or activities do give rise to the possibility of their attitude being read in that way.

Clearly the rationale behind the underground work of the ANC and SACP in South Africa bore some similarities to certain elite theories in that the vanguard element was supposed to have special qualities not found in conventional members of a political organisation. The vanguard element was expected to possess higher levels of discipline and willingness to sacrifice, and greater political understanding. They would be the ones with the capacity to choose targets with special political significance, or explain the vision of the organisation when requiring someone's cooperation or when charged with political organisation as one of the unit's operational tasks. This is not to suggest that these qualities were always found within vanguard movements, but that was the paradigm under which the approach was developed. Whether these qualities were actually found in the individuals concerned must have varied considerably from case to case. But they did have before them a notion of what was required from an 'advanced cadre', someone with capacity to conduct political and mobilising activity, to deal with the unexpected, to train, to decide whether to retreat or advance as required. But in other respects the notion of a vanguard was quite different from conventional definitions of elitism in that, despite an element of hierarchy in the organisation of the underground, it did not entail power over large numbers of people, nor was it distinguished by greater wealth (a conventional characteristic usually associated with an elite).

Nevertheless, modes of functioning did require initiating activities on behalf of others, or trying to stimulate others to initiate operations themselves. But, even if we concede that there was some elitism in the South African underground, we need to ask whether it was a precondition for stimulating later mass activity, or an obstacle:[21] was the elitism or vanguardism necessarily antagonistic to mass emancipation or emancipatory politics in the long run? Perhaps Lenin was right in thinking that outside stimulation by an 'advanced group' was sometimes needed to incite the masses to action. Evidence from the post-Rivonia underground suggests that the presence of 'elitist', 'self-appointed' underground ANC and SACP units did influence the direction of the 1976 uprising and was one of the reasons why many youths were later involved in the struggle under 'Congress hegemony'.[22]

In discussing elitism we have already mentioned the existence of hierarchical structures in the underground. Many of the activities of the units were military or quasi-military in nature, and this almost invariably implied a command structure. Underground operations in general, because of security and planning, required lines of command and hierarchies. But hierarchies and lines of authority, while they may have been operationally necessary, also provided opportunities for abuse, and could sometimes be employed to secure sexual or other favours. This appears to have occurred in MK camps in the preparatory phases of training for underground work, when commanders sometimes sought favours from younger women who were their military subordinates or in certain underground units; and the story may be wider in that much that happened may still be unreported (see Chapter 6).

The notion of underground, the space where dangerous, heroic acts occur, signifies an invisible area, a zone outside the vision of society in general. That is an essential part of the phenomenon – that it is out of sight, and not to be known about unless something is done that is intended to have a public impact. This is where acts of great virtue and historical significance for the advancement of liberation may occur or be planned. But at the same time, this is a situation which opens possibilities for abuse. It is precisely the conditions for underground success, secrecy and concealment of what is being done, that enable potential abuse to occur. It is impossible to gauge how much this happened. All we can say here is that the secluded, isolated, invisible space has more than one meaning and can host more than one mode of activity.

Today, one of the legacies of the hierarchical mode of conducting underground and military activity with distinct levels of authority is the notion of seniority, where people are accorded respect or even deference and are often described as 'senior comrades'. The basis for this notion of seniority is not always clear, though it often relates to having had command over others before, at some time that may be long past. It is sometimes said that once one has been a commander, those who were commanded always treat one that way.

As with many of these generalisations, they may be qualified by other considerations and by the effect of individual personality. Chris Hani, for example, sought to break down many of the tendencies to use hierarchies for abuse. Writing immediately after Hani's assassination, the late General Sipho Binda, a former MK camp commander, referred to Hani's interactions in Angola as MK commissar:

> His style of conducting political work was not bookish ... His first battle was to bring about humanness in the army. Harsh bureaucracy, poor administration, etc. were his targets. To us, who belonged to the officers' corps, we regarded that as the height of naivety. How can one bring liberalism and equality in the army? Emkhosini akulingwana (No equality in the army)!
>
> Bra Chris was not to be cowed nor discouraged by inertia or sheer reluctance towards change. He was not mincing his words. He wanted to transform MK into a real people's army. To him officers must be beyond reproach, women respected and given equal opportunities, and the rank and file well trained and motivated to engage the enemy at home.[23]

Conducting underground work required resources that varied according to the type of activities undertaken, where the unit was located or emanated from, to whom it reported, or where command structures were located. It often involved weaponry or sophisticated equipment, depending on the tasks. To supply or obtain these involved funding. Lack of such funding where it was required for subsistence or accommodation could endanger the existence of a unit, or lead it to suspend its activities. Sometimes the cheapest way of getting an item required for an operation was insecure and therefore avoided. In times of financial difficulty, the operative or unit might feel obliged to take the risk.

Where a unit was initiated externally or its funding was supplied from outside the country, accountability was difficult to ensure. Contact could easily be severed for a considerable length of time. Reporting to someone outside the country entailed great risks and could not be undertaken unnecessarily. It was hard to be sure that the person to be contacted would turn up at the assigned place, apart from other dangers involved in seeking the meeting. The operative might not go personally, and would have to send a courier, even though this entailed additional dangers by involving more individuals. Knowledge that one wanted to restrict was spread wider.

Communication by writing was very risky, especially if committed to the hands of couriers, who might be arrested. Codes were sometimes employed, but many of the coding systems were laborious to use and often difficult for some operatives to implement in the situation where they lived or worked. And many forms of coding depended on access to books and literacy.

The 'book code' was in common use. It may have derived from early Soviet training, and it was a painstaking task. Two people located in different places would agree on the book to be used and construct a message by indicating a page, then a line, then a letter in the line, each by number. For the word 'guest', one would have to count the number of letters in the line on a page of the book where 'g' was located, and then do the same for 'u', and so on. This took a great deal of time and in some cases became an emergency method only, used where the preferred method might have been intercepted and either the operative or the handler wanted to check whether there had been interception of communications. The preferred method may have involved some kind of chemically treated paper, or 'invisible ink', or more sophisticated ways of coding learnt by those who had received intelligence training in the Soviet Union,[24] and then 'inherited' by later operatives who did not undergo chemical training but were merely told how to treat paper, prepared by others, for sending or receiving.

Financial accountability in itself involved a whole set of problems. Given the secrecy surrounding the activity, the recipient of funds would use a code name in signing for any money. Over time even his or her exact identity would sometimes become blurred, especially in situations of the shifting deployment or even arrest of cadres and those who disbursed funds from outside. As different people took over responsibility for tasks, the links between the original recipient and disburser were broken.

Another problem arose when it became difficult to verify whether the activity for which funds had been disbursed had actually been carried out. Operatives sometimes sent reports of what they had done or claimed to have done but in many cases these could not be verified. The press generally did not cover activities of underground cadres,[25] and if what was claimed was fictitious there was little the handlers could do to establish the truth. According to one person entrusted with supplying funds to underground operatives, there were situations where the veracity of the reports received was dubious, and the funds provided might not have been used for the purposes allocated or for any ANC activities whatsoever. There were also situations where a person reported at both Swaziland and Maputo, seeking or receiving funding for the same project until discovered.[26]

While this account has highlighted the opportunities for abuse, it needs further contextualisation. In some cases the funds provided by the ANC were merged or kept with those of the operative. To do otherwise would have added complications and posed problems, given the requirements for opening formal banking accounts. If the operative were to have opened an account, it could obviously only have been a 'front'. One should not think of 'struggle accounting' in the same terms as recent fraud cases and ignore the real barriers standing in the way of the typical underground worker in the 1960s and 1970s. Operatives would usually work with hard cash since this money might be needed quickly. Probably most did not have bank accounts or cheque books (some ANC leaders received cheque books or credit cards for the first time in their lives only on election to parliament in 1994).

Where an operative shared a room with other people who were not involved in underground activities and had little private space, it was hard to keep documentation that could not easily be explained or whose character did not seem to gel with the surroundings. Finding a safe place for illegal activities was easier to imagine than to do. My personal experience in the 1970s was that I could never find somewhere other than my own home for preparing illegal pamphlets.[27] Obviously what could be done depended partly on the resources available. In a special mission, where substantial funds were left in a dead letter box or channelled in another way, a person or unit might be free to do things that were not possible for most operatives. But even having the money does not mean one can easily find a venue for some activity without arousing suspicion. If, for example, one hired a place purely for illegal purposes, this could alert others if it were not regularly occupied or used. A safe site for producing pamphlets, for example, was not necessarily safe as a place to live. What is apparently straightforward is often complicated in a world where minor matters could stir the interest or attention of others.

Thus it was not always possible to keep adequate financial records and ensure their safekeeping, given the diverse conditions under which people had to live, the limited opportunities they may have had for keeping records, and the skills they may or may not have possessed in such matters. Obviously the opportunity existed for the ANC's assets to become part of the private 'wealth' of the individual operative. But probably this did not happen in many or most cases; and sometimes the reality was quite different, as when people had to subsidise the movement with their own private resources. This was common because funding was difficult and could not always be timeous. On occasion it was politically important to act on a particular date or in response to some outrage or opportunity. Then people had to find the finances for their underground activities, sometimes receiving compensation later and sometimes (or usually) not.

The logistical difficulties in transferring funds made it more likely that operatives would use or seek their own funding in one way or another. If one was 'on the run' for organisational activities, ideally one should have been disguised and, if driving a car, able to change cars and accommodation. Yet many people sought by the police did not have access to these resources, sometimes not even a change of clothing, which made their identification and capture relatively easier. If they obtained a change of car or additional clothing, this expenditure to ensure their own security had to come from their own resources or through borrowing.

Certainly most did not have the resources to change cars or hire a car – assuming they had had the opportunity to learn to drive. On Chris Hani's first incursion into South Africa in 1974, the plan depended on his riding a bicycle at some point. Coming from a very poor part of Cofimvaba in the Eastern Cape where there were few roads and bicycles, Hani had never learnt to ride a bicycle and had to be taught by Joe Slovo.

Working underground, especially if completely underground, meant acquiring a new identity to disguise one's activity. This could mean adopting a particular lifestyle, which involved certain costs. Every time an operative bought a wig or a false moustache or new clothes or dyed their hair to change their image or had a car repainted in a different colour or hired a car, expenses were involved, but, again, compensation was seldom available.

The question of keeping records was especially problematic in the UDF, which in many cases had to operate semi-legally and could sometimes be regarded as part of the ANC-led underground while having to provide conventional legal accountability for funds. In some parts of the country the UDF operated illegally or semi-legally through most of its existence. This was especially the case in the bantustans or in areas with large concentrations of right-wing whites, like the Northern Transvaal. In that area, repression was more or less continuous from the mid-1980s and many of the leadership referred to themselves as 'internal refugees', as they continued to organise throughout the region.[28]

But travelling in a region that covered large distances required funds. Often receipts were not produced and Azhar Cachalia, the UDF treasurer at the time and now a High Court judge, experienced considerable difficulty because he had to report on the disbursement of funds. Sometimes, in conforming to the accountability that the UDF treasury required, the security of activists and their work was compromised. France Mohlala and a group of activists travelled throughout the region during the state of emergency and, as required, kept receipts of petrol and food expenditures. On arrest, the police seized these receipts and spent some days analysing them. Contrary to the modest account of their travels given by the prisoners, the police were able to produce a map of where they had been and when, based on these slips.[29]

Clearly there were contradictory modes or frameworks for operation, if one accepts that the UDF, when it functioned semi-legally, was a part of the underground. On the other hand the UDF was a formally legal organisation and there was the obligation to avoid unauthorised or unproven expenditure. The constitutional requirement of accountability for funds was enforced. Yet obviously the possibility of such forms of accountability was not intended to compromise underground work (though it sometimes did, as we have seen), which required modes of operation that were quite different.

These problems of accountability in disbursement of funds and the attendant openings for corruption have a legacy that can be seen in contemporary practices. On one occasion, when I was sent with a famous MK guerrilla to attend a conference, we were given a large sum of US dollars on the assumption that we would need it for accommodation and food. In fact we were hosted without costs and when I asked the MK comrade how we should calculate what had to be returned, his answer was that he did not see that anything should be returned. 'In the struggle you are given money for your mission, and that is for you to use.' Whatever the abuses, it is important to put them in the perspective of the broader picture, where conventional notions of accountability could not possibly have been implemented.

◎

An intrinsic feature of underground work was that some people knew more than others. It was part of the security of the mode of operation, that people ought not to know what they did not need to know. Underground operatives would often be tasked with providing intelligence on the character of and divisions within legally operating organisations. These reports would be sent, usually out of the country, preferably by some safe method such as chemically treated paper. The recipients were thus armed with information that could be deployed for factional political purposes, to advance one or other cause or to further personal agendas. They were then in a position to influence interfactional power by providing support to one or other faction, through the operatives who were to some degree accountable or interacting in a tighter or looser manner with them. The support could be that of endorsement by the ANC or SACP, to whose legitimacy UDF operatives within the country in the 1980s deferred almost universally, and also it could be in the form of resources provided by the ANC via various channels.

During the 1980s there were divisions between anti-apartheid groupings inside the country, each side claiming support of 'the movement'. It is hard to prove a direct link between these divisions and outside handlers, but it is true that certain underground groupings were established by or reported mainly to Mac Maharaj or Joe Slovo or Ronnie Kasrils or Thabo Mbeki, who, while not known to be directly involved with underground training, definitely had contact with individuals within the country. Many others must have reported directly or indirectly to Chris Hani, who operated extensively from Lesotho; but from what I know or have heard, he does not appear to have been connected to any of the groupings who were involved in these conflicts. The conflicts were mainly centred in the Transvaal, which may not have been Hani's area of primary focus.

In so far as some of these members of the National Executive were themselves in conflict, partly on a personal level, partly as a result of strategic differences, it is not unreasonable to speculate that they would use the operatives accountable to themselves to advance their own agendas. If this hypothesis is correct, more work needs to be done, difficult as it is to assess the information, on how certain groupings were funded, and on whose authority. Much of the funding came through Church structures but was initiated, as far as I know, by the ANC.

In the Transvaal, for example, there was a raging factional dispute in the 1980s between the well-funded, white-led group called Freeway House (the name of the building they owned) and others closely linked to the Transvaal Indian Congress. At one point in the mid-1980s I was in London and given access (after clearance by an NEC person, who was close to one of the leading NEC figures mentioned) to the list of recipients of funding disbursed by one of these individuals within the country. I saw that this was in large measure given to those associated with the Freeway House group. I am not suggesting that the person who disbursed the funds was consciously involving himself in factional activity. He may or may not have known of its existence. But in a situation where funds were scarce, for Africans in particular, it was possible for such funds to be used to create a relationship of dependence on the Freeway House grouping or any other that could provide funds for hiring halls or producing literature or transport. It is my view that a small number of groups in South Africa operated by creating these patron–client relationships as long as they were able. After some time that support for clients drifted away, especially as the insurrectionary climate of the mid-1980s developed and various debates about 'African leadership' became irrelevant with the emergence of militant activity led by African people in different sectors. (I omit various ideological distinctions between the factions, related mainly to an emphasis on the working class at the expense of national struggle or a combination of both. They are not germane to this study and may in fact have been subordinate to the desire to create patronage networks.) Both sides in the Transvaal were associated with specific African groupings and both claimed to be acting in accordance with the desires of the ANC or SACP leadership. While participants treated this as a dispute over strategy and tactics where higher authority was invoked to carry weight, it may well be that, paradoxically, both sides did make valid claims and actually enjoy support, but from different factions within the external leadership. It may be that both received resources from their backers, though I only know of one of these receiving the funding just mentioned.

Besides money, as we have said, knowledge was also a source of power. A further form of knowledge as power was obviously the role of some underground workers as intelligence operatives. The prevailing paradigm within the historiography of underground organisation places great stress on the supposedly overwhelming power of the apartheid state and its omnipresent network of informers. While this picture may be overdrawn, infiltration and other activities of apartheid spies were a real factor, inside and outside South Africa. The ANC therefore had to develop its own intelligence service. It is not clear how far it succeeded, but it does appear to have penetrated certain Security Police offices as well as the Home Affairs Department (thus providing false passports of the same quality as truly official ones).[30]

Having knowledge or the responsibility to gather such intelligence was an especially powerful weapon that could be used to advance the cause of liberation, defend the organisation from penetration, and also settle scores and fight in factional battles. The Hefer Commission inquiry arose from Mac Maharaj, leader of Operation Vula and later a cabinet minister in the first democratic government, and Mo Shaik, a former intelligence operative, alleging that Bulelani Ngcuka, then Director of Public Prosecutions, was an apartheid-era spy. The allegation was made on the basis of intelligence gathered or claimed to have been gathered during the 1980s, which was then put before the ANC. It could possibly have been acted on in that period, as was the case with allegations against Peter Mokaba, a former Youth League leader, and others who experienced a degree of marginalisation without the investigation ever being made public. Whether or not the allegations are true is not my concern here. What matters is that some individuals were deployed to gather information about other individuals, and this information could be used to confirm if someone was a spy and warn people to avoid the person or (as often happened) to isolate someone for other reasons.

Intelligence was received, purportedly always to enable the underground to take offensive or defensive action. But, as we have seen, it could easily be deployed for factional purposes and activity unrelated to liberation per se. There are also questions of a more general kind. Given the secrecy within which intelligence organisations operate and the ANC intelligence operated during the struggle, what determined when or whether information was used and how it could be employed? There are no clear guidelines for determining the conditions that justify making the data from intelligence sources known to others or in the current situation (then or now), to the public at large. If Ngcuka was a spy, why was the case put in the public domain only when certain individuals faced prosecution or were being investigated, including relatives of Shaik and Maharaj himself? At the time of writing, the dismissed former Director-General of the National Intelligence Agency, Billy Masetlha, facing prosecution, claims to have at his disposal information reflecting very negatively on highly placed individuals. He also refers to having played a role in the election of Thabo Mbeki. What are the controls that were placed on using this information prior to 1994 and later on, for dealing with opponents or advancing individuals whom one supported?

As for the underground operatives, not all or even most of them were intelligence officials. They may have prepared reports, but these were not specifically directed to the intelligence community. Here one must understand that intelligence or having intelligence in one's possession is an advantage at times, but also a burden. At the individual level, if someone knows you know something about them harmful to their career or credibility, you are in danger. More broadly, if you have a great deal of information and you are detained, what will you do if you are tortured? Sometimes people were questioned about one matter and held out, but after a long period suddenly told the police about quite different things. Even without being arrested, just knowing that one has all this information is a source of great stress.

It is important to appreciate the contemporary significance of this knowledge as a burden and not only as a power, as was used by Maharaj and Mo Shaik against Ngcuka. It may mean that someone in a powerful position knows that a particular individual knows this or that about him or her. This may be dangerous or it may prejudice the intelligence operative in one or other way. Much of this type of scenario appears to be playing itself out in some of the current politics in South Africa.

In seeking to protect itself from infiltration the ANC sometimes arrested spies or alleged spies. It has now been acknowledged to the Truth and Reconciliation Commission and in various internal but publicly available ANC commissions not only that innocent people were sometimes arrested but also that abuses occurred in the treatment of prisoners. It is by no means certain that all or most of those who were innocent have been publicly cleared. I have conducted an interview with one such person, who was held in Quatro and very badly tortured and later released without explanation. He returned to work for the democratic government after 1994 with some of the individuals who had tortured him. There has been no process of official clearing of this individual.[31] Many families know that the liberation movement to which they owe loyalty arrested one of their family. They are torn between their love for their family member and the belief that the organisation 'would not have done what it had done had there not been a reason'.

This chapter has presented a tentative characterisation of the main features of working in the ANC-led underground in South Africa. It has tried to show that simple labels cannot explain a very complex phenomenon. Underground activities led to different subjective reactions and actions on the part of operatives, some noble and heroic, others corrupt and abusive. The conditions under which people acted meant that the work of operatives could not always be observed or regulated by the organisation consistently enough to ensure definite and desired outcomes. But however one characterises underground activity, one has to acknowledge that its special conditions and circumstances had a direct bearing on the individuals and the organisation. At least two real questions remain to be answered. At a personal level, to what extent does the individual experience continue to have an impact on people's lives, and does it constitute a barrier to people's wellbeing and emotional fulfilment now and in future? At an organisational level, do the habits and practices of the past still persist in the present and are they obstacles to people's participation in the open, democratic society inaugurated in 1994?

6

GENDERING THE
UNDERGROUND

While this chapter is a start towards the complex task of gendering the underground, further research into these questions is needed for an adequately nuanced picture of the underground ANC's gendered character to emerge, within a wider inquiry on the formation and expression of both masculinity and femininity and notions of heroism. This continues to be an evolving area of research which requires careful understanding of its history, present context, and different meanings. There is not one script. Many people had diverse experiences. Rigorous work undertaken with great care is required to make adequate sense of these.

Existing general histories of the ANC and its structures do not foreground the gendered nature of this organisation.[1] It is true that in recent years there has been increasing attention to the rights and advancement of women in the ANC and society at large.[2] But in many of the works with a gendered approach the focus on organisation as a whole is not their main concern. The tendency is to look at aspects such as the status of women, and the evolving attitudes towards women and policies in general. While this body of work on women's history is indeed a worthwhile contribution in shaping our understanding of gendered interactions, it does not take us further in understanding the very core of the gendered nature of a political movement like the ANC. In many ways the patterns, cultures and identity of this organisation have been developed over many decades, and an unpacking and probing of the gendered culture of the ANC will go a long way to understanding the complexities of the past as well as those of the present.

Thus far there has been insufficient treatment of the ANC where men and women are seen as gendered subjects who have relationships to one another that are specific, historically conditioned and varied, indicating elements of subordinate or superior status in these contexts. The notion of women's rights may have been neglected for some time but its introduction without an adequate treatment of gender tended to see an equation of gender struggles with women's struggles, and the absence of men from such analysis. This conflation of gender equality struggles and struggles for women's rights has resulted in a lack of nuanced understanding of the complexity of gender interactions and culture within the ANC organisation.

It is necessary, therefore, that if one says that men and women are interacting, this be understood as comprising a specific male–female power dynamic, often mediated by other factors and changing over time. The literature of the underground element of that history tends to erase women or their experiences in gendered relationships,[3] and indeed some scholars have asked what it has to do with such a study: why should I include it in a work like this?[4] While making explosives is seen as relevant by all who are interested in the underground, gender is supposedly only for the few. However, this work probes the very gendered assumptions and conditioning that subjects such as explosive-making bring with them.

Elaine Unterhalter has indicated that the role of women is sometimes recognised and their bravery acknowledged, but they are not treated as operating in gendered relationships that entail distinct social dynamics;[5] yet women who are brave are not 'substitute men' doing what men usually do. In the 1980s there were incidents where women were given recognition after detention or imprisonment and it was often said of them *uyindoda*, 'You are a man.'[6] Although, of course, this was said in an affirming manner, it does give a glimpse of how people see the public political space and its gendered nature. This naming of the experience is one facet of the privileging of one gender and its experiences and erasing what it meant to be a woman in the struggle. It also gives a glimpse into the general tendency of liberation discourse to be masculinist and (as we shall see, for specific reasons) to elide recovery of freedom with restoration of manhood.

Liberation struggles are often seen as essentially defined by masculinist discourse, an essentially male and public terrain where women periodically enter. This chapter considers how men, in the special conditions of subjugation and denial of manhood found in South Africa, reacted and interacted with women within a liberation movement and how other factors mediated this relationship. The underground is a distinct place of interaction and consequently influences the character of the gendered relationship in ways that are by no means uniform, just as the women and men react in more than one way.

To see the place, role and nature of gender contradictions, it is helpful to study the specific intersections with race, class and other factors made salient primarily by apartheid rule and also changing conditions within the ANC over time, within particular geographical areas and modes of activity. The gendered relationship is not something pure or abstract that operates universally in one form. The surrounding power relations mediate the meanings of concepts so that they often carry connotations and qualities quite different from what they would in other situations. Even the notion of patriarchy has a range of meanings and manifestations, and that is especially true of its collision with colonial and apartheid structures, which have undermined or interfaced with and sometimes restructured the phenomenon in a range of ways. Gender relations and dynamics in the ANC have changed through time and are varied, depending on where they happen, and with the militarised and general underground components obviously operating with specific modalities that are substantially different from others.[7]

Much of what is discussed here bears a relationship to the key gender-dynamics question, that of the interaction between the public domain – the place where men are 'supposed to be' – and the private one, supposedly reserved for women. The assumptions of this dichotomy tend to consign women to the household, their entry into the public domain being seen as bearing an anomalous, unnatural character or being in a manner that replicates the notions of woman as homemaker – a view that has been described as 'public patriarchy'.[8] It consequently tends to meet with resistance or be undermined in varying ways, and this is true of the ANC and the ANC underground, as we shall see. Patriarchal power is played out in a distinct terrain, within pre-existing and changing cultural contexts.

Given the implications and lived experiences of oppressed African men and women under apartheid and colonialism, they bear some qualities in common with gender relations universally but also have a specific character related to the denial of African manhood. The African nationalist struggle asserted African manhood, among other things, in the same way that for African women the notion of 'motherism', the emphasis of the place of women as mothers in struggle, dominated the public discourse on self-assertion. It is true that much of the discourse in African nationalism has evoked masculinist imagery, but there is a complex terrain of women's self-representation and much effort needs to be made to locate and modify or qualify meanings. These are shaped by decades and indeed centuries of experience where most of what is seen as attaching to manhood has been denied. Unfortunately, some of the limited literature discussing manhood in the South African liberation struggle does not take its surroundings into account and thus reads off meanings entirely from words. While not denying the power of words, what they signify requires a reading that situates meanings in the deep and broad body of experience that has led to their articulation.

In her reading of the mode of self-representation, Natasha Erlank quotes words that are masculinist but does not connect these to the actual denial of African manhood. Furthermore, she attributes exaggerated strategic significance to this masculinist language:

> In 1935, Alfred Bitini Xuma ... wrote a paper expressing confidence in the ability of Africans to participate responsibly in governmental politics because of their having come to the 'status of manhood'.[9] In 1946, Anton Lembede, leader of the ANC Youth League, wrote a charged newspaper article describing how a 'young virile nation' was in the process of being rebirthed, drawing strength from a nationalism which fed on the idea of Africa as a 'blackman's country'.[10] Xuma and Lembede were not alone among African nationalist leaders in resorting to rhetoric saturated in references to masculinity, although their vision of what it meant to be a man may have differed. Language redolent with metaphors calling for the reassertion of a denied manhood had prominent rhetorical place in nationalist discourse in the first part of the century. Seldom acknowledged, the existence of this discourse is *fundamental to understanding the political strategies of the ANC and other nationalist groups from the 1920s through the 1950s*. Such a discourse explains some of the gendered currents that motivated nationalist activity during this period as well as some of the reasons why African male leaders were disinclined to involve African women in political activity.[11]

Erlank traces a documentary history whose discourse continually refers to emasculation and the need to restore manhood and a virile nation. Unless it is contextualised, it is historical in the sense of chronology, but ahistorical in that it fails to locate these assertions fully. This masculine idiom is also, of course, the male-dominated language of the time, not only within African discourse or only in liberation movements.

Notions of a hierarchy of gender power take on different meanings in colonial and apartheid states, where manhood is actually assaulted – where men are called boys no matter what their age, or where many whites never even bother to know their actual names.[12] This infantile status was expressed very plainly by General JBM Hertzog, South African Prime Minister in the 1920s and 1930s:

> Next to the European, the Native stands as an 8-year-old child to a man of great experience – a child in religion, a child in moral conviction; without art and without science; the most primitive needs, and the most elementary knowledge to provide for those needs. If ever a race had a need of guidance and protection from another people with which it is placed in contact, then it is the Native in his contact with the white man.[13]

This is a mild example from the genre of racist writings of that time. What it signifies is that the infantilisation of Africans, men in particular, links to or seeks to justify political domination by designating Africans as a race of children. There are variants of such discourse – for example, the use of terms such as tutelage, trusteeship, sacred trust and others. All these terms refer to native people not having attained adult status, requiring a long phase of evolution to understand the responsibilities of adulthood or not having any prospect of becoming an 'adult race'.

Given the linkage in colonial discourse between denial of manhood and African political freedom, African assertions of manhood need to be understood not only as a challenge to a putative childlike status but as symbolising wider rejection of overlordship, represented by such statements as Hertzog's. The assertion of manhood is in this context a claim for freedom. It is a statement of personhood that may or may not have any implications for women as such.

Colonialism and apartheid consciously set about subduing the military power and perceived sexual threat of the African male. The latter finds repeated expression in nineteenth-century colonial commissions where reference was made to African men leading lives of 'indolent sensuality'. Because they battened in ease on the labour of their wives they did not fulfil their 'proper destiny' and work for the white man.[14]

Colonial and apartheid authorities tended to let 'traditional' processes of transition to manhood continue. This stance may require explanation. We know that the culture of the Other was treated as exotic and that it was marginalised in relation to that of the coloniser. Even where some colonisers purported to value local culture, it tended to be treated primarily as an anthropological curiosity. Western music, art and other practices constituted the only culture of universal validity. Their African equivalents fell within the realm of anthropology.[15] This is in line with notions of indirect rule and overall conceptions of control by asserting the inferiority of Africans in the territorial realm physically occupied by the colonisers, coexisting with the idea of maintaining the cohesion of the 'traditional', for which some colonial powers purported to have great respect.[16] The social order and the social discipline provided by that order were part of what made it possible to rule colonies with relatively small numbers of colonial officials. In that sense, perpetuation of a variety of indigenous customs, including initiation, sometimes helped maintain and perpetuate that order (and was also sometimes part of the threat to the same order).

African men were related to in two quite separate modes within the colonial encounter and in the areas falling outside their policing and direct control, which led to the playing out of patriarchy in at least two distinct ways. Manhood has been conceived from early times as including a right and duty to protect.[17] It is inherent in the notion of the housewife and mother caring for the home and the man protecting his 'castle'. He is often designated as a warrior partly because he has to protect his home from attack. He is also seen as the person who works so that the woman can perform her household duties.

But the notion of protection and the concept of patriarchy to which it is attached should not be given one universal meaning, irrespective of context.[18] In the apartheid era the notion of 'protection', seen as one of the qualities of manhood, was in one sense what one might normally attribute to 'patriarchy', and also performed beyond the apartheid terrain, in other countries and contexts. But because of the conditions under which it was acted out in South Africa, its meaning was often qualified and its parameters circumscribed in ways that did not 'protect' women but in fact reduced their rights and level of protection below what had been enjoyed in precolonial societies.[19] Apartheid and colonialism invaded relations between husband and wife, and father and child. That was itself a situation which often left men feeling that they were not able to protect 'as men', and was therefore humiliating.

The MK veteran Matthews Ngcobo describes his father being humiliated before his eyes by the police and the entire notion of his power within the family being undermined:

> There was something that ... started to worry me – there were searches ... Then when you are a child you always think your father is very powerful, but when you see your father being harassed one day by other men, you see that there is something wrong. You see that you miscalculated. Then you realise that, no, my father, there is other power that is beyond him – because when these police come at night they're forcing, they kick the door – he doesn't fight ... So that was the worst humiliation that I experienced in my life when I grew up.[20]

There are also other types of cases, for example where police arrested an activist daughter and a father was powerless to intervene – fearing the worst for his child but also losing his role as protector.

> The police came to our house. My cousins and I had come from the river with water buckets on our heads. As it was dark I could easily slip away and not reach our homestead. But I knew that someone in the village must have told the authorities that I was around. So I went home to where the police were waiting. I knew if I did not pitch or disappeared in the dark my parents would take the blame. At home the cops said they had a warrant for my arrest. My dad protested, he was upset and he was angry. I knew that his intervention would lead to violence. It had happened before. So I stepped up and said, 'Tata, let me handle this.' 'You are a child,' he said, 'let me deal with this.' Mom and I exchanged glances. I read the pain in her eyes and she must have read it in mine. But we both knew here was a power larger than anything in our living room. The police had their R1 rifles ready. They were

menacing, edgy and I knew they would hit Tata. I got up, between my dad and the police, and said, 'Tata, *ndizakibuya*' – 'I will come back.' Let me take these people and their dogs which were waiting outside the house away from here.

He held me briefly and I felt the rage and the powerlessness in his hug. There were other kids, cousins, and they were scared. So I got a bag and, in the dark, got in the police van. The dynamic between the 16-year-old daughter and the father had shifted more than what lay ahead. This was the most fearful thing. For the first time, I noticed the spot of baldness – just a patch on my father's head – as I came out of the house [and] he was waiting at the bottom of the veranda. I got in the van and he held the door after it was closed. It was but a moment – his forlorn hand remains imprinted in my mind forever.[21]

The overall argument presented in this chapter is that one cannot read gender relations or a negative relationship of men to women from the assertion of manhood alone. Manhood acquires complexities which it does not have in conventional Western societies or which it had in precolonial societies. The power dynamic changes it all. But even without this background John Tosh, writing of nineteenth-century Britain, goes so far as to claim that such statements are in the first place addressed to men:

Although all codes of manliness laid down the lineaments of proper conduct towards women, that was never their prime concern. Manliness was fundamentally a set of values by which men judged other men, and it is a mistake to suppose that those values were exclusively – or even mainly – to do with maintaining control over women ... [T]hey had little to do with the upholding of patriarchy. The prevalence of manly discourse is as much about homosociality as about patriarchy. [22]

This chapter tries to probe the multilayered and multifaceted assertion of manhood. From the research it is clear that the assertion has no self-evident and timeless meaning, nor the meaning attributed to it in writings which purport from such discourses to read notions of gender inequality and even broader political strategies.[23] Indeed these assertions and self-identification of forms of manhood may and often do entail unequal gender structures, as well as patriarchal domination. But it would be remiss not to probe the complexity and dynamic meanings and potential scope of such evocations.

The male–female gendered relationships should generally be analysed as an issue distinct from manhood. Even where the concept of the nation was implicitly defined in terms of manhood, as in the original ANC restriction of membership to African men, it coexisted with extensive political and public activity by women in a range of demonstrations. Women immediately entered the public terrain,[24] and in practice even played a role in the ANC itself, long before the constitution formally admitted them as full members.[25]

The struggle to be a man meant more than masculinist imagery. It was essentially the struggle for dignity and the reclaiming of rights to be treated as an adult human being. This is something that needs to be read into any analysis of ANC masculinities and femininities.

Given the saliency of manhood claims, it is not surprising that there is also evidence that the national liberation movement connected in some cases with actual processes of transition to manhood. Notions of initiation to manhood, used loosely, are often found in the practices and language used in various terrains of the liberation struggle. The language of denial of manhood coexists with that of regaining manhood through the struggle or struggle-related activities. Mongezi Radebe recalls:

> I know, for instance, people in Heilbron whom I had never thought were politically aware, and I got friendly with one and he gave me *The Struggle Is My Life* by Mandela, and he said it's a good book, *it'll make me a man*. A man selling coal ... I had never thought that he had been to school, and I knew him not to be in a position to read anything or write his name, but he gave me that book. So it was like that in townships all over.[26]

The act of joining ANC or MK was associated in some situations with attaining manhood or undertaking rites of passage. What is entailed in initiation is controversial, embracing a wide range of rituals, and inviting potentially contested meanings. It is important to understand how initiation or its values, in the context of national liberation, interfaced with and sometimes differed from 'traditional' notions of manhood. The interface between masculinities and the struggle was extremely varied. In some ways it linked the imagery it drew on to earlier pre-Union notions and values of manhood connoting martial bravery. In other senses it connected with age-old practices, originally requiring specific rites of passage in order to achieve manhood. Peter Delius has suggested that Pedi initiation processes stressing a warrior tradition facilitated recruitment to MK.[27] In situations where the warrior notion of manhood persisted, it certainly could be of assistance in recruitment for armed struggle. The late Zingiva Nkondo, when asked why he joined MK, indicated that the Shangaan, an offshoot of Shaka's Zulu kingdom, were 'always ready', by virtue of their history, to embark on military activity.[28]

Initiation arises in a more complex manner in the former Western Transvaal (now the North-West Province), where the community of Dinokana, at the time of the Rivonia Trial, emerged from a period of intense resistance against the imposition of passes on women. Some of the chiefs in the community had sided with the women and the ANC against the authorities. This alliance of patriarchs and women reveals the ambiguities already referred to, namely an assertion by men of their power over and protection of women, but simultaneously a desire to avoid humiliation and powerlessness in relation to a state that could harm their wives and daughters.[29] The chiefs set up underground structures, which they linked to MK and its recruitment machinery. According to Radilori John Moumakwa, who was one of between fifty and eighty boys aged 14[30] who were sent to Bechuanaland (present-day Botswana) to join MK, they were told that it was time to 'bolwa' or 'bolala' – that it was no longer the responsibility of their fathers to provide them with trousers.[31] According to Dr PM Sebate of Unisa's African languages department, the context and meaning of initiation would suggest that in this case it would be completed through joining MK:

What 'go bolala' means here is that the boys had to go out to be initiated in the teachings of MK so that they could be men amongst men … Having graduated as MK soldiers, these boys would be able to protect their families, villages and above all their nation. These boys will be in the forest … They will be there for the three winter months, where they will be taught work songs, war songs and hunting songs; and that a stick thrashing can only kill an ant. [Then], when boys from Dinokana went out to join MK, they were between childhood and manhood and were tasked to go out and learn 'war songs', to protect their nation, that the 'whipping they received from the white man could only kill an ant'.[32]

MK may have provided elements of what was required in their transition to manhood, in teaching war songs. This can be seen in the words of the following song played on Radio Freedom:

Abasakwazi Nokuphumula (They Cannot Rest)

lead *Bayekeleni, sobabamba ngobunyama*
chorus *Nangokuhlwa*
lead *Abasalali, umkonto, mkonto wesizwe*
chorus *Abasakwazi nokuphumula*
uMkhonto uzobashaya, uzobaqeda
lead *Mabesati bayagalena*
Sizofika sifuna, uMkhonto weSizwe
chorus *Ushona ngapha, ushona ngale,*
Bayawazi.

Translation: Let them be. We will get them when it's dark. When night comes they cannot sleep, due to the spear, the spear of the nation they cannot rest. Our army will hit them, we will finish them when they try to do one thing or the other, the people's army will come. Here now, then there – they learn of our elusive forces.[33]

In the case of Dinokana, conventional rites of passage had been disrupted because the chiefdom felt under pressure from the white authorities. The apparent acceptance of rites, involving recruitment to MK, was meant to prepare boys for manhood and the ensuing responsibilities of defending their chiefdom and its women. Similar processes have been recorded more recently in the case of Palestinian youths, where episodes of conflict with the Israelis and imprisonment were treated as replacing normal processes of attaining manhood. As a result generational hierarchies were disrupted within Palestinian families and youths returning from prison were treated as men enjoying greater seniority than their own parents.[34]

In the Matatiele area of the former Transkei, it was the element of secrecy attached to initiation ceremonies that formed the basis of recruitment to an underground unit. The experience they had shared as part of an initiation group enabled those already selected as MK members to assess the suitability of others and decide which of the rest of the group should be recruited; and the secrecy which linked them as a group was seen as crucial in establishing themselves as an underground unit.[35]

It is not clear to what extent initiation practices were implemented in exile. In Solomon Mahlangu Freedom College, established by the ANC in Tanzania, South African *ingcibis* (circumcision doctors) were available for those who wished to be initiated. But, according to Dr Siphokazi Sokupa, the boys were not taken to live in the bush for some time as the tradition required. It was feared that in tropical surroundings so different from the veld of the Eastern Cape, students would develop diseases like malaria.[36]

It appears from informants and interviews as well as literature on Robben Island that many young men demanded to be initiated, though this is not well documented for those in exile. According to Johnson Malcomess Mgabela, who practised as an *ingcibi* outside prison in the Eastern Cape, he circumcised 361 prisoners on Robben Island as part of an initiation process.[37] While some accounts and most individuals are silent on the content of the notions of manhood communicated alongside circumcision, there was a group of older men who carried out these responsibilities.

Such initiation, occurring under *de facto* ANC auspices, often leaves unstated what precise notions of manhood were entailed, what meanings were commended to the initiates. That boys were circumcised signifies little, for this is an operation that can occur outside initiation. It is by no means clear that notions of initiation within South Africa follow any one pattern;[38] what traits are commended to boys as desirable for a man in the instruction and lectures they are given before and after circumcision may vary considerably. It seems that both on Robben Island and in exile initiation tended to embody a liberatory content, a distinct conception of manhood drawing on the values of the struggle. This was the case in exile in the initiation of Chris Hani and Sandile Sejake, now a general, formerly a leading MK soldier who did reconnaissance prior to the Wankie campaign.[39]

It should be cautioned, however, that this was in exile, within a military situation, and would tend to predispose manhood to be understood within the notions of military valour and association with war. Likewise most of the MK prisoners operated with a similar mode of thinking and expectation of their future life. There would be less room for variations which might encompass sides of manhood that stress gentler versions of masculinity. Nevertheless, from glimpses of Oliver Tambo in exile and Walter Sisulu in prison, some of the dominating figures representing these other forms of masculinity, there is no doubt that they would have had elements of such exposure, if not during the initiation itself, then during their experience as a whole. Within the context of warfare and the heroic element entailed in such activities, these teachings could have had some impact on imagery that the young men associated with being a soldier, and much that is evoked is gender-related.

◎

There is a romanticism attached to underground and military activity, in some ways like espionage or even gangsterism being seen as exciting and dangerous by many people, where heroism can be savoured at a distance or can inspire others. The notion of heroism is starkly gendered, associated in conventional dictionaries with man; and the word heroine derives from the male form. Clearly the hero is seen as an essentially male figure. No doubt many elements of liberation activity were dangerous and therefore called for heroism. And it was gendered in that it was assumed to be primarily man's work – and, as Unterhalter shows, the people embarking on a heroic project, exemplified in autobiographies she analyses, saw their part in the struggle as 'real work', unlike their conventional work to earn a living.[40] This is the same distinction we find between public and private work, where a man may be seen as the breadwinner and a woman as the homemaker. There again, the concept of work is not applied to work in the home; all work, including heroic work, is the prerogative of the male.

In South Africa the heroism of revolutionary activity lay in challenging a regime that was often depicted as omnipotent, beyond any form of contest by those it oppressed. The heroism was manifested in a range of ways, some very dramatic, as when MK soldiers, as people who were not allowed by the state to possess guns or undergo military training, attacked police stations and destroyed other apartheid targets. Others engaged quietly in secret activity, ensuring that the message of the ANC was heard even when it was supposed to be silenced. Some of the most heroic of these quiet actions happened within repressive government structures; unbeknown to the public, they promoted the liberation movement. Julius Fučik (later executed by the Nazis) saw the same thing in occupied Czechoslovakia.[41] What is clear is that many who performed heroic deeds are unsung and may never be known because they worked in secret or under cover of doing something else.

The concept of heroism cannot simply be embraced without noting some of its ambiguities. As we saw in Chapter 5, its zone as a place of danger is a potential space for both noble and abusive activity. In the case of underground activity it almost invariably takes place outside the public vision, in seclusion or where what happens is not visible, a setting well suited to both liberatory activities and abuse. I am not saying that abuse was common, but I know that it did happen. In so far as there were serious cases in the underground, they would have been very difficult to unmask: conventional reporting to the South African Police would expose an underground unit.

The heroic project links itself to a received historical tradition which ties the freedom struggle to previous generations of those who resisted conquest and oppression. Both Mandela and Sisulu have said that early accounts of resistance to conquest influenced their decision to join the liberation struggle. This is a theme that was aired each night at the beginning of the Radio Freedom broadcast. The discourse establishes the male warrior as hero in ANC self-identity, a model of manhood to be emulated. In conducting the armed struggle, cadres were encouraged to see themselves 'picking up the spear' that had been dropped when Bambatha and others died in the last armed rebellion before Union, in 1906.[42] They were continuing a tradition of martial heroism and resistance.

One of the key figures in this iconography is Makhanda, sometimes spelt 'Makana' ('He who grinds maize'), who led an attack on the garrison in Grahamstown in 1819 and was sent to Robben Island, where he died while trying to escape.[43] Interestingly, discussion on that conflict is expressed in the language of manhood, confirming a continued linkage between heroism and masculinity. After Makhanda surrenders in order to save his people from further loss of life and their crops from further destruction, councillors approach the British. In their statement they say their 'fathers were MEN' (capitalised in original transcript), relating this to loving their cattle, wives and children and holding their property.

They wanted peace but not on condition that they submit to Ngqika, the ally of the British, with whom they had been at war. Interestingly, not only do they call on the British to let Ngqika 'fight for himself', but they conclude by saying that 'you may indeed kill the last man of us – but Gaika [Ngqika] shall not rule over the followers of those who think him a woman.'[44] This is an early illustration of the theme that manhood is associated with willingness to resist, to defend one's land and people, children and womenfolk. Honour was associated with being a man. The depiction of Ngqika as a woman was an image of cowardice and treachery.

When Mandela, Sisulu and Radio Freedom invoked this heroic male tradition there was some erasure of the involvement of women as warriors, one of the most outstanding being MaNthatisi of the Tlokwa, and women of many other peoples, notably the Zulu.[45]

By definition, the warrior tradition includes a readiness to deploy violence where necessary, a readiness to die but also a capacity to wound or kill. The heroic readiness to die is captured in notes made by Nelson Mandela, in preparing for the death penalty to be imposed in the Rivonia Trial, where he stated that he should be known to have died like 'a man'.[46] One of the many aspects of a warrior tradition is that booty is seized, spoils of war are taken, and rape sometimes occurs. Thus Keeley, writing generally of a variety of precolonial societies, argues that the

> capture of women was one of the spoils of victory – and occasionally one of the primary aims of warfare – for many tribal warriors ... In situations where ransom or escape were not possible, the treatment of captive young women amounted to rape, whether actual violence was used against them to enforce cohabitation with their captors or was only implicit in their situation.[47]

Many people in some parts of the Eastern Cape are clearly the offspring of such encounters. Historians speak of Khoi and San communities becoming absorbed into Xhosa-speaking peoples.[48] There were also various forms of unfree labour where San were compelled to stay as workers. It may well be that a description of such a relationship is that the women in such situations were 'absorbed' as wives. But the reality often is that in some or all instances they were first captured, so whatever followed was one element of a power relationship premised on coercion. The sexual and other relationships in such a condition were by definition without consent (as in slavery). Motsei shows much in the Bible, a major influence on many South Africans, indicating condonation or approval of taking women as booty.[49] Mazrui argues of precolonial Somali society that almost any weapon of war becomes a phallic symbol, that there is an intimate association between combat and sexual conquest. War dances acquire both sexual and martial suggestiveness.[50]

There is thus no denying that the warrior tradition, the militarist tradition, entailed not only heroic acts but also many cases of abuse and power over women including forced marriage to a member of a more powerful group or outright rape without marriage. Rape is named as such, but marriage amounted to the same thing where it resulted from victory in war.

The object here is not to foreground rape or abuse within the notion of being a warrior, but merely to indicate that this may sometimes happen when a person acts as a warrior or as a soldier (as is the case in many parts of the world at this very moment).[51] The heroic and warrior lineage cannot be accurately conveyed unless it includes this.

Reciting the general history of the struggle in South Africa is an important way for people to locate themselves in it. In autobiographies of men Unterhalter points to how this history was constantly being repeated, which she at first found somewhat tedious. But she later came to believe that it was part of the individual's need to link himself within this longer tradition, to place himself there, continuing that revolutionary saga which had a past and a future that he would play a part in realising.[52] This phenomenon is also communicated where more experienced comrades tell of the conduct of those (almost invariably) men whose conduct was considered exemplary. The young cadre was exhorted to learn from Moses Kotane. Even Walter Sisulu, himself an 'exemplary comrade', cites the authority of Kotane when dispensing advice: 'I am a firm believer, like Moses Kotane, in discipline. An organisation is not governed by anger. It must be governed by analysis by examining the situation and not mechanically.'[53] What these narratives do, according to Unterhalter, is that 'in forming a "grand narrative" they cement the existing accounts and orderings and characterisation.'[54]

Unterhalter has identified a common construction of masculinity found in the writings of men of all races, classes and generations, which she describes as 'heroic masculinity'. The male hero conducts his active life in the public realm, where he develops deep bonds of friendship with other men; he is supported unquestioningly by his wife or mother or girlfriend, who occupies the private sphere of the home. 'The sacrifice of "the soft world" of feminised relationships is justified in terms of the "hard achievements" of heroism and male camaraderie.'[55] Unterhalter also shows how male activity in the struggle is depicted as the 'work of the struggle', in that sense treating their conventional work, whether as architect, labourer, or doctor, as a minor element of their lives.

This depiction of underground work as mainly the activity of men who left women behind to look after the children and other household duties is borne out, for example, in the autobiography of Ben Turok. Returning home after he had placed a bomb at the Rissik Street post office,

> Mary [his wife] asked me what the matter was and I was not able to tell her, but she knew that I was on edge. When she read the newspaper the next day, everything became clear. She was rather resentful at not having known about my MK role and we discussed this. *Certainly, she had to pay as high a price as I did. She had previously been left with the children while I was in hiding and she had to face the police when I was away. But our security demanded this kind of balance and she was bound to accept the arrangement.*[56]

While there are many similar accounts, the playing out of male heroism was in fact complex and varied. The legendary heroes who inspired Mandela and others, as well as the practices of those whose autobiographies are analysed by Unterhalter, do not represent the only model of manhood and heroism found within the ANC. As we shall see, some of those conventionally regarded as 'heroes' of the struggle had quite varied and different ways of playing out their masculinity and heroism. They sometimes conducted themselves in a manner that flouted the stereotypical notions of what constitutes a hero. We therefore need to be extremely wary of casting notions of heroism within a monolithic model. Moreover, as we shall also see, the 'heroic project' was never confined to men. There were women who were themselves soldiers or underground workers – part of a heroic project – and in some cases these women had men under their command.[57]

Then again, indicating further complexity, Ray Alexander joined the Communist underground while her husband Jack Simons refused, to some extent reversing the conventional playing out of the public sphere and domestic responsibilities.[58] This was a pattern in their marriage: Jack, a leading theorist, would drive Ray to her trade union negotiations and wait in the car, having to content himself with his books, a flask of tea and sandwiches.[59] Without pretending to provide a comprehensive view, we can see that there were simultaneously different conceptions of manhood found in the ANC and that there were many men as well as women who did not conform to the conventional heroic masculine or supportive female role found in the works that elucidate a notion of heroic masculinity.

◎

In considering the diverse models of manhood, we should reiterate that the ANC has never treated or examined itself as a gendered organisation, nor have the general histories of the organisation; and there has been no self-examination of manhood within the ANC, and only a limited amount in academic studies. Yet this is a topic that deserves interrogation. The political predominance of the ANC means that understanding its gender practices and notions of manhood may be one of the bases on which gender equality will have to be grounded in the future. Through their conduct, some men like the Makhandas of the past represented models of manhood that were commended to others, much as the Cubans say, 'Be like Che [Guevara].' Many people no doubt conformed to macho militaristic images – military activities encourage traditional notions of manhood. But there were individuals, some of them famous revolutionary figures, who did not conform to these conventional notions, men like Chris Hani and Vuyisile Mini.

Mini was a SACTU leader, an early MK soldier, Communist and composer of revolutionary songs, including the famous 'Nantsii Indodemnyama Verwoerd! / Vorster Basopha nantsii Indodemnyama!'

('Watch out, Verwoerd/Vorster! Look out, here comes the black man!').
He died on the gallows, convicted on false evidence. Cadres used to
be told stories about Mini being offered his freedom on death row in
exchange for supplying information about his comrades, and refusing.
In the tradition of freedom fighters 'holding their heads high', Mini is
said to have walked his last steps singing some of the many freedom
songs he had composed.[60]

These are the qualities often associated with being a revolutionary
and in particular with 'revolutionary masculinity', found especially in
someone like Che Guevara or Chris Hani. The oral and written tradition
of a liberation movement tends to create a model of what revolutionary
conduct is and to identify the people that are its exemplars, part of the
stock that individual revolutionaries referred to in locating themselves
within a struggle history. Clearly Mini has been projected in this light.
But there was also a side to Mini that is not so easily assimilated into
this convention.

Sobizana Mngqikana, as a member of the Border Regional
Command Secretariat, was instructed, after MK was formed in 1961,
to write to comrades in Port Elizabeth demanding a report-back on the
ANC conference held in Lobatse in 1962. In some ways this mode of
operating was a hangover from the earlier period of constitutionalism
with its normal forms of accountability, without sensitivity to the
changed conditions demanded by illegality. Mngqikana reports:

> In response to our demand a delegation comprising Vuyisile Mini and
> [Caleb] Mayekiso[61] came to East London. The meeting lasted from
> 8 p.m. to 5 a.m. the following day. The four-room house in which we
> held the meeting was discreetly guarded and secured by MK cadres.
> Before we could delve into the main part of the meeting, Mini, in tears,
> expressed dismay at the uncomradely letter we had written. 'Did we
> know the implications of the resort to armed struggle?' he asked. 'Did
> we appreciate that blood is going to flow and that lives are going to be
> lost?' At some stage he couldn't continue as tears rolled down his cheeks.
> Mayekiso, I remember, mildly reproached him: 'Vuyisile, Vuyisile,
> stop this, stop this!' After a while he cooled down and proceeded to
> give a report of the Lobatse conference and the expectations that the
> leadership had of us.[62]

Here a revolutionary hero did not behave according to conventional notions of manhood, where men are not supposed to shed tears, that being the role of wives and widows. It contradicts the idea found in much masculinist discourse that the rational is the prerogative of males and the emotional that of females.[63] In this case, Mini provided MK soldiers and members of the ANC with a model of manhood that disrupted conventional military expectations of what manhood entailed.

Chris Hani is another heroic personality who broke the mould. The model he presented is especially important because he has attained a heroic status somewhat like Che Guevara's in the Cuban struggle. This is not to suggest that Hani and Che were saints. But there is a complexity in Hani's life and a definite break from conventional notions of the male hero that need to be factored into any account of masculinities within the ANC, as we shall see below in considering his reaction to abuse of women and his general approach to gender issues.

Another caveat is that conventional macho conduct does not seem to have been uniform among the rank and file, although the evidence remains limited. Faith Radebe gives an account of male soldiers' longing to have children visit the camp in Angola. She reports that they continually asked that Angolan women be allowed to visit the camp with their families so that they could have children around them. In the same camp men objected to the fact that pregnant women were sent to Tanzania to have their babies because of the facilities available there. They wanted the women to give birth in the camp and asked for similar facilities to be provided there. They longed for elements of 'normality' in their lives, like the presence of babies.[64]

While we need to question a monolithic view of the heroic male, we should also examine the precise nature and scope of the role and status of women in the ANC underground. The role of women in national liberation movements appears to be controversial very often, as is the place they occupy after liberation. One debate surrounds the character and extent of their participation compared with that of men: did they engage in active combat or were their roles of secondary significance in military terms, and what significance is attached to the question and its answer? Secondly, the question has been raised whether or not women's involvement has tended to reproduce patriarchal relations found in the country or society at large. Thirdly, there is debate about the compatibility of women's involvement in revolutionary work with feminist doctrines. This is advanced in a number of ways. The fact that women have often entered liberation struggles initially as mothers has been seen by some as immediately disqualifying any feminist significance in their action, and as automatically and comprehensively reproducing patriarchal relations.[65] Another argument is that participating in a liberation struggle tends to subordinate and ultimately displace feminist demands in favour of 'larger' nationalist ones. It is also claimed that the military efforts of women tend to have no effect on their status after the war, and this idea seems to have proved true in many such struggles.

Existing literature has tended to dismiss or downplay the involvement of women in political struggle. It has been suggested that the ANC was reluctant to place women in dangerous situations, especially in combat, and that women were thus not effectively or properly employed as soldiers. Instead, this view continues, they were confined to supposedly less dangerous work as couriers or in communications, surveillance and reconnaissance; or, at the furthest extreme, they participated as 'mothers', supporting the role of men, or in other respects performing conventional female roles. All these factors were said to qualify their claim to be part of a revolutionary struggle in a meaningful sense. The problem with this approach is that it presupposes a narrow, formal definition of a combat role. It also fails to recognise the significance of supportive, logistical and intelligence roles as integral to the success of military operations. Even giving a meal to a soldier or providing shelter for the night before an engagement converts a conventional maternal action into a key element in the war effort.

Totsie Memela was a MK cadre, a lot of whose work involved reconnaissance, the type of activity described as less 'glorious'. Yet what she did appears to have been just as dangerous as the actual infiltration of the Vula group for which she prepared, having to ensure the safety of every point at which they entered, and every place where they would stay. In her developing role one sees how an MK woman gradually grew in skills, responsibilities and confidence. Her work entailed smuggling arms into South Africa and placing these in dead-letter boxes (DLBs),[66] where they could be picked up by fighters. Memela describes how her expertise grew:

> And as time went on I had gone ... for training in Angola, and when I
> came back then I was able to go and actually prepare DLBs, actually put

guns and be able now to write maps for people to be able to come and pick that up. Pick those things up and know more about DLBs and how do you make sure, where do you put the information for people to know where the dropping has been. How do you make sure that you've put the signs so that they can be able to see where you've actually dropped the guns? And some of the times I would get specific people that I'd been told to go and give the material to. I would have to make sure that I have cleared my route, I understand what's going on to make sure that I don't get arrested, and later on starting actually infiltrating people, comrades, from outside.

I kept on graduating in terms of the responsibilities ... but the bulk of the time my role was infiltration, which started from a simple letter and later on I was now infiltrating or taking people outside the country, groups of people. At the time, for example, when in Natal there was quite a bit of violence, I used to take out students and I would come inside. And I was coming into the country illegally [initially she used to do ANC work while entering legally]. I would come into the country ... make the connections and ... take out these groups ... because I had quite a huge network in Swaziland. And then I would take them to ... safe houses and ... send them through to Mozambique for all sorts of different things, for example Bheki Cele [MK cadre, now KZN MEC].[67]

Routes had to be checked in every case, knowing patterns of roadblocks, and getting information about any change in them. Legends had to be developed to explain the presence of individuals in parts of the route, should they be discovered. Means of communication were required to know whether they had arrived safely or not.

Just how many women like Totsie Memela participated in the underground struggle is difficult to determine. According to Jacklyn Cock there was a dramatic increase in the numbers of women soldiers after 1976. By 1989 they made up approximately 20 per cent of MK cadres.[68] Whether these figures are accurate or not depends on one's basis for counting – on how one defines a combatant. Personally, I believe they only embrace those formally inducted, whereas MK activities in fact involved far more people than its enrolled foot soldiers. The contributions of women are more likely to be invisible or unacknowledged than those of men, when such calculations are made.

There is no doubt that women were present in significant numbers in the overall military effort involving MK, albeit generally as a minority.

They were formally recruited as members of underground units or MK, or participated at a less formal level, performing a variety of tasks more or less close to the actual military action. Working underground and going to war against the apartheid regime as they did, women substantially disrupted any notion of the struggle as a 'heroic male project'. As one woman soldier observed, 'We lived in the same camps. The women did exactly the same training as the men. Exactly the same. Drilling, handling weapons, topography ... everything.'[69]

Yet women's participation took place under conditions initially set exclusively by men, who determined the extent to which their roles were limited or enhanced, encouraged or discouraged. One cannot make bald and unqualified assertions since the situation was often complicated and contradictory, and the responses of both men and women were by no means uniform. Moreover, women's involvement in the underground took place at a time when the gender consciousness of the ANC as an organisation was taking shape. In the 1960s and 1970s feminism was still a contentious doctrine within the ANC and notions of gender equality were only gradually emerging. Many sections of the predominantly male leadership accepted the restrictions on deploying women to 'more dangerous work', although there were some significant figures like Chris Hani who challenged the confinement of women to stereotypical nonmilitary roles.[70]

In our army ... when we came in, women were deployed mainly in ... communications, in the medi-corps or in the offices. Comrade Chris challenged that. We get the same training but we are deployed differently. It is unacceptable for the people's army. Women should be deployed anywhere they are trained for and he used to be the key person in trying to get women to come into the country [as guerrillas] because his view was we are all trained for combat duties but women tend to get involved in combat-related duties, not in combat itself, though they get the same training as men.[71]

Just as the leadership's views were not monolithic, so the experiences, impressions and reflections of women from this period convey more than one message and interpretation. Some women felt their male comrades did not take them seriously, undermined them and considered them a threat. Women often felt excluded by male camaraderie. As one noted: 'And you could see some of the things that you're not involved in. It's only men, who stand there whispering. And then they're gone; and you start asking yourself, Why am I being left out?'[72] Given the continued persistence of gender stereotypes, women had to struggle for full recognition as soldiers. Referred to individually as *umzana*, a pet name meaning 'small house', which incidentally was also used in tertiary institutions to refer to women's hostels,[73] they were given types of work that fitted the label, or so it is claimed.[74] Then again, it was sometimes assumed initially that women did not come to join MK or go into exile out of personal conviction, but to follow a male lover. Thus Shirley Gunn was asked, 'Whom are you following?'[75]

Others, however, have reported more positive experiences.[76] Jacqueline Molefe, now General Sedibe, claims that women through their actions earned the respect of men in the army and were treated as equals.[77] Faith Radebe also did not experience men as undermining her or other female members of MK; in fact they were pleased to have them as leaders in particular situations.[78]

Within the underground units and in the MK camps, problems also arose on sexual bonds between men and women, especially when these cut across the military hierarchy. Many women formed relationships with senior figures. It was sometimes suggested that women were attracted to these men because of their ability to provide more of the good things of life in a harsh environment or because they were more likely to be more mature and experienced than male trainees of a similar age group to the young women.[79] Tensions then arose with the male soldiers with whom the women worked. Some commissars, while admitting the right of the women to form relationships with senior men, advised them to be discreet and treat the relationships as private and conduct them out of the public eye.

Because women formed a tiny minority of soldiers, they were particularly vulnerable to the unwanted attentions of older and senior men. Chris Hani took steps to prevent senior officials taking advantage of new MK women. Dipuo Mvelase reports:

There was a situation where in our army there were very few women and they come into the army, officers will jump for them, all of them and use, or misuse their powers and the authority that they have to get women. That led to some nasty situations. Comrade Chris established this Rule 25 – it was a new rule – that no officer will have a relationship with a new recruit because it is an unfair relationship. A recruit needs to be given a chance to know our army so that they can make a decision about these things and understand ... things because when they come in people use their authority and the difficulties of training as a soldier, to start relationships with these women and the rule was a problem with officers. But not that they could defy Comrade Chris. Though, I mean, people complained about it. But it was observed.[80]

If a woman fell pregnant she was generally sent to Tanzania because of the facilities offered there. This not only separated partners but also interfered with or disrupted the woman's political work. Some women insisted on being able to continue as fighters or taking part fully in other activities and appear to have won these rights, because childcare facilities were provided in Tanzania, able to house the children in the event of the mother being posted elsewhere.[81] These women had struggled for the chance to continue fighting and in most cases that meant leaving their children behind. Shireen Hassim quotes an MK cadre as saying, 'I didn't need to choose between motherhood and politics because the Women's Section made it possible for me to do both. I knew I could leave my child in good hands.' However, on the basis of one other source, Hassim claims women did not want to leave their children there. Being prepared to leave a child in the care facilities is described as a 'minority view' by Hassim, and 'most women ... in the movement were unhappy about being separated from their children'.[82] What is most strange about Hassim's account is that after elaborating on the problems allegedly associated with the ANC crèches, she claims that women in MK were not allowed to become pregnant.[83]

Clearly women did not want to leave their children, but they did want to fight; being able to continue fighting after giving birth was a gain but one that generally required their children being in an adequate care facility. This is a complex position to find oneself in and even now, so many years after liberation and 'normalisation' of life, unresolved issues still remain which many families continue having to find ways to deal with. They have to address the previous history of separation and, indeed, balance this with the fresh demands of building a new social and political order while themselves settling together as a reunited family, where that is the case. There are a number of underground fighters who returned to the country in the 1980s and felt compelled to try to send their children to safety outside the country because of the dangers of their work. Exile, with all its problems, was seen as offering better opportunities and safety for their family. Many married couples in the struggle found that their marriages could not bear the strain of continual separation. It was sometimes difficult to be together at moments of personal crisis or illness, for example. In one case, the divorce was not a result of longstanding problems but derived directly from the demands of the organisation. This was accepted as the cause and did not lead either party to renounce their commitment to the struggle; but it was a price demanded, as was the case with mothers who had to leave their children.[84]

Not all women left their children behind. Some were able to take them on their assignments, even when they worked underground inside the country. On occasion, having a child provided a better cover for these operations in that a mother with a child appeared less likely to arouse the suspicion of her being a trained MK soldier.[85]

Besides sexual relationships of choice, rape, sexual harassment and other abuses undoubtedly occurred. Their extent does not appear to be quantifiable on the information currently available. While some women report harassment, others never encountered it.[86] There are definitely recorded cases.[87] Thus Mashike records an interview with a former MK female soldier: 'When I remember my first three years in exile, I feel like crying because I had sexual intercourse with more than 20 MK commanders. I also saw this happening to other young female comrades who joined MK in the 1970s and 1980s.'[88]

How wide the extent of abuse or inappropriate or unequal sexual relationships was cannot be established, but in the wake of the Jacob Zuma rape trial there are women, who had not previously publicly voiced their experiences, who indicated such abuse. No doubt this kind of incident was underreported and in many cases loyalty to the ANC would have made some women reluctant to reveal their experiences. The absence of adequate mechanisms for protection and legal remedy would also have deterred some women from laying complaints. Even in the 1980s, within above-ground struggles, it was hard for women cadres in the UDF to seek a remedy for rape because of the illegitimacy and distrust of the police. To have approached the apartheid police to report such a crime would have been unthinkable for most UDF women.

Some form of redress was sought through organisational structures, with varying degrees of success.

As we have indicated, the notion of a hero and especially a military person is associated primarily with men, and the military is a male institution par excellence. One of the questions that arise is whether the price for women of working in MK and the underground was a degree of masculinisation. While the South African Defence Force maintained a hierarchical ideology of gender roles and cultivated a subordinate and decorative notion of femininity, Jacklyn Cock cites one informant as finding irksome 'the egalitarian ideology of MK [which] sometimes involved a denial of femininity'.[89]

Sometimes, when women did what was required to succeed in the army, they claimed they evoked resentment from some of the men. This was by no means a universal experience. In fact, as Cock's and my own research has shown, the experiences of women were not one and the same. Asserting femininity in this context refers to doing what a woman might wish to do outside the military context, particularly dressing in a particular way, wearing make-up and similar choices. For some women it was important to assert this side of themselves in addition to their identity as a soldier, but they often felt frustrated – success in MK tended to limit that form of self-expression. For other women this was less of an issue; they had other ways of expressing (or refusing to assert) their femininity.

It seems that many women enjoyed weekends when they could wear conventional clothes and affirm their womanhood in a way akin to that 'at home', and not be purely soldiers. A uniform, designed as it is to override or even deny individual identity, went a long way to restrict people's self-expression. One informant describes an image he remembers from a camp, where Thenjiwe Mtintso emerged from her tent wearing a mini-skirt, with a pistol in her belt. He admired her beauty; that was part of the normal life for which they longed.

So did women have to pay a price in joining MK, either by contesting their right – as they saw it – to be women as well as soldiers or suppressing something of their own femininity in order to be accepted? In other words, was there a 'masculinisation' of women, the adoption of modes of behaviour that conformed to a militarised conception of masculinity in order to win acceptance?

There is nothing unusual about such a phenomenon.[90] Even if feminism and notions of gender equality were consolidating within the ANC over time, there obviously would remain gaps between the consciousnesses of various people. To this day norms of gender equality are unevenly diffused within the ANC and society at large. That much is well known. Consequently, many men when seeing women succeed in the military would have perceived this as a claim on 'social power' within a terrain that they regarded as a male preserve. This would provoke some antagonism.

Antagonism to women entering this terrain also showed when women played roles that were not conventionally designated as female – even for women joining the underground – and they were depicted as misfits. This was how Barbara Hogan and Marion Sparg were portrayed by the white media and judicial authorities. To them, because the idea of a white woman identifying herself fully with the cause of the oppressed (mostly black) people of South Africa was in itself abhorrent, identification as an underground worker and especially as a trained soldier, in the case of Sparg, was particularly repugnant to the white male view of what should constitute femininity. Faced with such an attitude, for some women the only way of reconciling what was irreconcilable in their understanding was to deny their femininity.

Returning to the earlier question of whether the price for women of joining MK or working underground meant 'masculinising', on one level this could be answered through a survey of how various women perceived their experience. Unfortunately that degree of access has been impossible to attain.

However, one can address the question in another way by asserting the reality that all people have multiple identities. Even as a soldier, one does not cease to be whatever else may constitute one's identity, even if the elements may be repressed or underrepresented at times. A good example of this quality comes from a photograph by Margaret Randall of a 16-year-old Sandinista woman soldier. Dressed in military uniform, she has a rifle on her shoulder, wears a huge cross round her neck, and in her shirt pocket there is a pen and a nail file. The caption reads: 'Somewhere in Nicaragua this sixteen-year-old woman defends her country ... with a gun, a cross, a nail file and a pen.'[91] This quotation from Nicaragua captures what has also happened in South Africa. Women entered the military world with multiple identities. Some of these were in abeyance at various times and were only acted on at particular moments, just as in Nicaragua, where this young soldier could attack the 'Contras'. She may write poetry. She may read the scriptures and at moments of leisure will care for her nails.

In the stressed work of a revolution, inevitably parts of one's personality tend to be repressed, and people in the underground experienced this – men as well as women. For operational reasons one's desire to be with one's lover may be interrupted. One may be sent far away to do the business of the revolution. It seems that most operatives accepted the need to pay this price and suppress their personal needs (see Chapter 7). That does not mean that the desire for normal life or the life that one hoped to enjoy in a democratic society was limited or obliterated. It had to wait, as something most revolutionaries still hoped to enjoy.

◎

This chapter has argued that the liberation struggle threw up distinct models of manhood based on a notion of heroism suffused with ambiguities. Some of these models fell within the tradition of the heroic male warrior. Others broke this mould and confounded conventional expectations and practices. All were, however, contingent on conceptions and practices of femininity. This presence of widely differing models of manhood, and of womanhood, within the ANC underground means that the stereotypical qualities conventionally attached to 'male' and 'female' need extensive qualification.

7

REVOLUTIONARY MORALITY AND THE
SUPPRESSION OF THE PERSONAL

This chapter deals with the relationship between the individual and the liberation movement as a collective. There are a number of distinct factors that bear on this relationship; at the same time, they are all connected to one another and are phenomena that need to be treated in their own right. The notion of the collective has an impact on individual judgement, personal choices and intimacy, with its concepts of the organisation as family or parent and a tendency to displace interpersonal love by 'love for the people', displayed through one's revolutionary activity.

Much of what has been written in the last two chapters has a bearing on what it means for an individual person to participate in a revolution. The relationship between a revolutionary organisation and the individual – raising the question of the 'personal' – has a direct impact on individual conduct and individual judgement.

The imperatives of the organisation can curtail the freedom of the individual to do certain things that people in an open, democratic society can do without question. The relationship also has implications for the family, for personal relationships, and for the individual's emotional life, by providing a context for both the fulfilment and repression of emotions. The consequences for the social, intellectual, moral and emotional lives of those involved are complex and profound, and form the subject of this chapter.

Revolutionary thinking in the ANC was much influenced by Marxist texts of Soviet origin. One of their premises was that revolutionaries were supposed to realise themselves as individuals within the context of the collective.[1] While few were able to meet these demands, there were exemplary figures like Chris Hani, Bram Fischer and Ruth First[2] who were willing to sacrifice their lives for the popular cause and realise themselves in the service of something much bigger than themselves. They provided models which others were urged to emulate. But, noble as such lives may have been as examples, they also embodied elements that created problematic choices and results in the personal lives of many of these revolutionaries.

Two of the ways we can consider this relationship between the personal and the collective are how it affects the individual's judgement and how it affects personal and intimate relations with others. For many people the way this has led to problems is evidenced by the many broken marriages or having to deal with the after-effects of long separations in intimate relationships. Some developed a modus vivendi that enabled them to meet their duties to the revolution as well as personal needs and obligations to other people with whom they were close.[3]

While the bulk of the chapter is devoted to notions of love and the personal generally, it begins with the impact of belonging to a revolutionary organisation on one's right to one's individual judgement. Then for the rest of the chapter we turn to the question of the personal in relation to individual needs being displaced in the context of 'love for the people' and related perspectives.

Conflict could easily arise between individual judgement and the imperatives of the organisation. Typically in revolutionary situations, once decisions of the collective are arrived at, they are binding on individuals, who may have argued contrary views in the process of debate leading up to the decision. (This is not peculiar to revolutionary situations, of course, but is also found in conventional caucuses of contemporary democratic parties.) During the Russian Revolution, for example, those who had opposed a decision were often later selected as the individuals who should implement it.[4] This is part of the notion of 'democratic centralism' – though it has been said that there tends to be more centralism than democracy. The assumption is that the more open a situation, in the sense of freedom of political activity in the society at large, the greater the internal democracy prevailing within the party. On the other hand, the greater the degree of repression in the society, in particular where an organisation is illegal, the more the centralised element comes to the fore. Paradoxically, after the SACP abandoned democratic centralism as an organisational principle in the 1990s it reappeared in ANC documentation in 2000 and is now asserted as a central element of the ANC's and apparently also the SACP's mode of functioning these days. This was the case before Thabo Mbeki's defeat in the ANC presidential election in December 2007 and appears to continue under Jacob Zuma.

Obviously the notion of responsibility to the collective, while necessary in many ways for the survival of a revolution, and especially an underground organisation, carries with it the possibility of abuse, as well as that of entrenching a culture of resistance to fresh thinking and innovation. The pressures and security considerations of a protracted underground struggle may make individuals and organisations especially resistant to much-needed changes of approach. One can only wonder how much more difficult it would have been for the SACP to adapt its strategic thinking, had the collapse of the Soviet Union and its allies occurred when the Party was still operating illegally underground. In that situation, innovation and periodic rethinking were less prevalent than the transmission of a body of accepted ideas which cements the unity of the organisation.

The central question that we are considering, that of the individual judgement versus the collective, is highlighted in an episode related by the ANC MP and former SACP leading member Ben Turok in his autobiography. During the 1973 Durban strikes, Turok was in contact with Harold 'Jock' Strachan, a former political prisoner, who sought funding to assist those involved in the trade unions.[5] Turok tried to obtain Party support and appears to have received an unsatisfactory response to the effect that structures inside the country would handle the situation. Turok had doubts about the security and efficacy of SACP underground work and decided to pursue methods of operating outside the organisation. He managed to raise funds and channelled them to Strachan. When the SACP discovered this, he refused to divulge the names of the people to whom he had given the money, believing it would endanger their security. The SACP, in turn, considered it unacceptable that an individual member should act in this way without accounting for their actions to the organisation. Turok was expelled.[6]

Some members have in retrospect maintained that Turok was expelled for 'good reasons'.[7] Within the paradigm that the SACP espoused, it was plainly unacceptable for a member to operate independently, running a private funding operation for activities inside the country. On the other hand, one has some sympathy for Turok if, as he claimed, he did not get an adequate response from the organisation and did not have confidence in its security. What should he have done? From my experience as an operative in the Durban area at the time, security seemed to be good in the range of activities where I was involved. No one did anything that placed me in unnecessary danger – but I operated on a small scale. In so far as the underground existed at that time, it does not appear to have gone beyond a scattering of small units. There was unlikely to have been the kinds of organisation and resources in existence to provide the facilities Turok needed. While MK groups entered the country from time to time, these were sporadic and do not seem to have established enduring structures that Turok could have drawn upon for support and assistance. Whether Turok was right or wrong in taking the action he did, he nevertheless put himself outside the SACP collective, and he should not have been surprised at the action taken.

This discussion is not intended to pass judgement but to show that when one problematises the relationship between the individual and the collective it raises issues that need to be considered within the paradigm of the particular activity. One can make a case both ways. A similar though more recent example, in the context of an open democratic state where the dangers of illegality are not present, had a different outcome. In 2002 Jeremy Cronin, Deputy General Secretary of the SACP, conducted a long, two-part interview with the Irish academic Helena Sheehan which appeared on the Internet. In the course of the interview he referred to the possible 'Zanufication' of the ANC, meaning that the ANC might take a decadent, bureaucratic and undemocratic course as had happened with ZANU in Zimbabwe. This statement evoked outrage among some members of the ANC leadership and some semi-racist responses describing Cronin as a 'white messiah'. While the substance of what he raised was not debated, his wording was regarded as a vilification of the ANC and, having been raised outside the organisational collective, was treated as impermissible.

When the matter came to the National Executive Committee of the ANC, a suggestion was made that the Communists meet in a separate caucus. This group advised Cronin to apologise. According to the paradigm within which Cronin worked, he was subordinate to both the ANC and SACP collectives and he therefore saw fit to apologise. Many have referred to this as a 'craven' apology and 'cowardice'. In some situations it is true that bravery may be measured by whether or not an individual stands against a collective, and speaks 'truth to power'. But in this case Cronin saw himself as duty-bound to subordinate his own private judgement to the demands of the collective.[8]

It is interesting to ask whether the primacy of this paradigm is conducive these days to the development of democratic debate within the organisations of the liberation movement and democracy as a whole. I have a number of ambivalences. To the extent that organisations like the SACP may have changed or even renounced some of their previously pioneering positions on gender equality (in the Jacob Zuma rape trial),[9] which had inspired many people, since there is no situation of danger now, it would seem to be one's duty to speak one's mind or leave the organisation. It is said that where individuals disagree with certain positions that they see as flying in the face of the organisation's heritage, they should fight to win them within the organisation. At a certain point, having failed to restore the democratic and non-sexist heritage of the organisation, is the collective not becoming a cloak behind which individuals shield in order to retain certain positions, with various actual or potential benefits?

Democratic centralism – under whatever name – is not peculiar to Communists or the ANC. In reality all organisations, and all party caucuses, demand a degree of subordination of the judgement and will of their members. It is a feature of party discipline almost universally. It is all a matter of degree and many factors need to be brought into any judgement that an individual takes.

At the same time, when I originally wrote this chapter, the situation was less stark and divisive than it now appears within the ANC and its allies, who have just emerged from a national conference (December 2007) which has been engaged in contestation not over ideas so much as for spoils that would come from one or other person becoming leader and probably the next State President. In short, ideology and programmatic issues have been supplanted by personal support and patronage.[10] Democratic centralism has little to do with this crisis or with its potential resolution. The centralisation of government rule under Mbeki is found throughout the continent and is not related to any notion of democratic centralism.[11] The crisis is unrelated to forcing views on people in the name of a collective, for there is a range of collectives within the ANC and its allies at present and their differences are not clearly ideological. Throughout much of 2007 it was a question of winning support for Zuma or others, a politics without programmes.

Returning to the period when subordination to a collective was a viable consideration in the sense of a recognised collective leadership existing, whatever moral judgement one may wish to make, we need to be aware that there are conditions and circumstances under which the individual's judgement needs to be subordinated to that of the collective. Having entered that relationship, the individual knows that is the case. In a revolutionary situation such as prevailed in South Africa in the 1960s, gathering momentum until the late 1980s, this kind of subjection was necessary for the ANC's and SACP's existence underground. Whether conditions prevailing in the twenty-first century make it equally necessary is open to question and, as indicated, perhaps impossible to enforce in the current turmoil. All paradigms relate to a context and, in so far as that context changes, new paradigms need to emerge.

◎

Any involvement in a revolution has an impact on conceptions of the personal. Given the overriding demands for sacrifice and loyalty to something greater than oneself, it leads invariably to a negation of intimacy. Indeed there is a substantial body of revolutionary literature which exalts a conception of personal sacrifice for the revolution as the highest and most honourable duty of a revolutionary cadre. In the words of Liu Shaoqi, notes from whose work 'How to Be a Good Communist' were found in Nelson Mandela's handwriting at Rivonia, here is one example from this genre:[12]

A PARTY MEMBER'S PERSONAL INTERESTS MUST BE UNCONDITIONALLY SUBORDINATED TO THE INTERESTS OF THE PARTY. At all times and on all questions, a Party member should give first consideration to the interests of the Party as a whole, and put them in the forefront and place personal matters and interests second … Every Party member must completely identify his personal interests with those of the Party both in his thinking and in his actions. He must be able to yield to the interests of the Party without any hesitation or reluctance and sacrifice his personal interests whenever the two are at variance.[13]

Here, we see the idea of a revolutionary as an individual who expects nothing personally, who is prepared to sacrifice all personal needs in order to ensure the success of the struggle.[14] Consequently, no sacrifice is too great and there is no situation where personal needs can supplant those of the organisation. Ernesto 'Che' Guevara, whose exemplary life inspired generations of revolutionaries throughout the world, carried these ideas further in their implications for personal and emotional life. Speaking of the demands on revolutionaries he claimed that the revolution demanded every hour: 'The circle of their friends is limited strictly to the circle of comrades in the revolution. There is no life outside of it.'[15]

Though it may have been very exacting, such single-mindedness as he presumes may have been necessary for the successful conduct of the tasks of a revolutionary and also helped to blot out some of the personal pain entailed in the sacrifices being made. The denial or curtailment of the scope of the personal was generally one of the conditions for the successful prosecution of revolutionary activities. We need to acknowledge this, not least because of the consequences, including scars, that have been left through these sacrifices; they should be recognised and if possible remedied.[16] As WB Yeats wrote in his profound but ambivalent poem commemorating the martyrs of the Irish Easter 1916 rising, 'Too long a sacrifice / Can make a stone of the heart.'[17] Such numbing of emotions is part of the legacy of ANC-SACP underground activity, for these conceptions of revolutionary morality were more thoroughly absorbed in the underground than any other site of struggle.[18] There are sacrifices, beyond those that are known, that remain with many people, unacknowledged as part of their contribution.

Underground work and its secrecy forced people to make hard choices, involving enduring pain and guilt for many. A significant number of people had to leave their homes, families and loved ones, usually without informing them of their departure.[19] At the time, the expectation was that they would soon return; instead, many were absent for decades, unable or afraid to come back in case this put in jeopardy the security of those left behind. A particularly stark example was the sudden departure of Eric Mtshali to join MK in 1962 without his being able to inform or say goodbye to his wife or children. Eight years later, without having had any contact or opportunity to explain his reasons for departure, he learnt from casual conversation with sailors in Dar es Salaam harbour, that his wife had died.[20]

The question one may ask today is what the consequences were when spouses or children were not consulted about the decision to leave.[21] Such consultation usually did not take place; if it had, it may well have endangered the activities of MK. Obviously this left much 'unfinished business', which often remains unresolved to this day. In many cases families did not hear of their children's or other family members' decision till much later. They sometimes expected them to return with material wealth, while instead they often returned without means of support and became dependants, a burden on their parents or other relatives. This exacerbated earlier resentment caused by their original disappearance (as various returnees have told me in their first-hand accounts).

Many left children as babies only to see them again three decades later.[22] Anton Qaba explained how – because of security considerations – when there was a call on someone to leave for MK work, there was no such thing as 'I have left this or that at home.'[23] Hilda Bernstein captures and summarises the pain of exile, borne mainly by women, well:

> Exile exacts its price not only from those who leave, but also from those who are left: ... often without a word of farewell and leaving behind no money for material needs. The women went to work and brought up families alone and in loneliness ... often through silent years without any communication from the one who had left ... Many who left concealed their intention to depart from those closest to them.
>
> ... Then their lives were haunted by the unresolved departure – not having said goodbye ... Without the rites of farewell the one who had departed was already within the realm of the dead ... Abrupt and secret departure added a sense of guilt to the exiles' pain of unresolved separation from the closest members of the family ... The years of loss and suffering of the mothers are only one part of the picture; the other is the alienation, the resentment and feelings of rejection suffered by the children who were left behind.[24]

In the case of Ruth Mompati, who was sent out of the country for political training in 1962, she was not able to return because it was believed she would face arrest. This forced her separation from her children. 'But I still wanted to go back, because I'd left a baby of two and a half years, and a child of six years. And I just couldn't think of not going home.'[25] When the family did reconnect in 1972, they did not know one another. 'I was not their mother ... I was a stranger ... I think I suffered more, because they had substitutes. I hadn't had any substitute babies. I now had grown-up children, who became my children as years went on.'[26]

Though Guevara's exhortation may seem to require a level of commitment that few would be able to match, harmonising personal and political needs was not impossible, and in some cases was achieved despite the great stresses. The example of Albertina and Walter Sisulu is well known.[27] The Sisulus' responsibilities to the 'ANC as family' do not seem to have impaired their conventional roles as parents and grandparents or the exercise of their responsibilities to children and grandchildren. In fact, Walter Sisulu was constantly consulted on Robben Island about the naming of children or other family issues. In the case of Albertina Sisulu, her role as mother cannot be narrowly confined to that of a caregiver or whatever other conventional notions attach to motherhood. She also saw herself as a politiciser of her own children and caregiver to a wide range of others whom she embraced as 'sons and daughters'.[28]

Success in underground work meant that operatives had to harden themselves and repress basic needs to communicate with others. The work meant concealing important parts of their lives and fears and anxieties. Often this created misunderstandings in not meeting social expectations from people or simply failing to explain adequately why one or other thing was done or not done. Underground life sets serious limits on social and emotional life.

◎

Paradoxically, both Liu and Guevara do not deny the importance of love. But in the revolutionary context, they do not conceive of or acknowledge love as an interpersonal phenomenon. Personal love is supplanted by 'love for the people'[29] and, as we shall see, this often also connects with a notion of the liberation movement or Party as 'family' or parents. Guevara writes:

At the risk of seeming ridiculous, let me say that the true revolutionary is guided by great feelings of love ... Our vanguard revolutionaries must make an ideal of this love of the people, of the most sacred causes, and make it one and indivisible ... The leaders of the revolution have children just beginning to talk, who are not learning to say 'daddy.' *They have wives who must be part of the general sacrifice of their lives in order to take the revolution to its destiny* ... We must strive every day so that this love of living humanity is transformed into actual deeds, into acts that serve as examples, as a moving force ... In our case *we have maintained that our children should have or should go without those things that the children of the common man have or go without, and that our families should understand this and struggle for it to be that way.*[30]

Ray Alexander Simons described how she was unwilling to return to Latvia whence she had emigrated as a teenager, in order to join her fiancé, because 'although I was not in love with any other man, *I was indeed 'in love' with the people here,* the country and the struggle against race discrimination.'[31]

◎

Participating in the struggle entailed a distinct notion of 'family'. Writing of the Spanish Communist underground, Guy Hermet refers to the Party as 'a sort of extended family in which memories and hopes are shared and to which [the member] is tied both emotionally and materially'.[32] In South Africa, Communists sometimes used the word 'family' as a metaphor or code word to refer to the Party.[33] This was also true of the ANC. One woman cadre, in explaining to her children that she had to leave them behind in Tanzania in order to carry out an ANC assignment, told them that 'although I may be your mother, your real mother and father are the ANC. The ANC will look after you, feed you and clothe you.'[34] This conception is part of a continuous ANC cultural phenomenon long predating the period of illegality. This is seen in recollections of the role of volunteers in the Congress of the People campaign, which led to the adoption of the Freedom Charter. Mrs Sibanda, an old volunteer from Cradock, reported, 'Whenever we went to people's houses, and they were in trouble, or had problems, we would become mothers of that family, and men volunteers should be fathers.'[35]

The notion of ANC being *in loco parentis* arose also in the context of cadres wanting to marry.[36] Permission had to be sought from the ANC leadership before a couple could marry. Security considerations made contact with family back home difficult if not impossible, and placed strain on young couples who felt uncomfortable with taking the step to marry without the knowledge of their family. Baleka Mbete argues that the need for the organisation to approve was not a sign of authoritarianism but a responsible attitude, ensuring that adequate investigations were conducted to ensure that other parties were not prejudiced, for example undisclosed spouses left behind in South Africa. There was also an overall need to care for young people who left in their teens and had no role models to learn from or depend on.[37]

Many young people longed to see their parents, and the organisation was depicted as performing a similar role. While it could be parental in some ways, it could not fill the gap. In fact, many young people missed their parents very much. Phumla Tshabalala speaks of missing her mother every night. But it was not only the young girls or women who longed to have a parental void filled. Gertrude Shope, head of the ANC Women's Section, was asked to visit camps for two days instead of one because so many young men wanted to be with a motherly figure.[38]

Muff Andersson, a former MK cadre, has been quoted as saying that the ANC 'had no mechanisms to help members cope with depression and anxiety. "Women felt they could not even talk about it. There was a fear that if you acknowledged these feelings you might be seen to be weak and less dependable for revolutionary work."'[39] It may well be that the mechanisms for coping with psychological problems were generally inadequate, but it appears that this is not the only experience that needs to be built into our understanding. As a revolutionary, Chris Hani appears to have departed from the 'revolutionary masculinist' norm, which sees men as bearers of the rational, the emotional being the preserve of women. Soldiers, notably women in MK, testify that Chris Hani made cadres feel that their personal fears and emotional make-up were as much the concern of the army and the revolution, as strategy and tactics. Dipuo Mvelase, a female MK commander, describes the way in which Hani raised issues that for many people were outside the bounds of revolutionary discourse:

He was ... a comrade to whom you felt you can say anything and not feel bad about it, whether it is personal or whether it is about the struggle ... Someone you could confide in, probably say certain things that I couldn't even say to my mum ... Despite the fact that everybody needed his attention because he was the commander in that area [in Angola], we had about three hundred new recruits and he spent every single evening talking to us. And you felt wanted, you felt at home. You felt important you know. Asking you about your family, how you feel, what is your experience, do you miss home? Questions that you thought you wouldn't be asked because we are in a revolution ... you as a person, you get lost ... But Comrade Chris made sure that you don't get lost ... He humanised the struggle ... He made every one of us feel we count. This is something that one never experienced before, because there are those big expectations that revolutionaries have to do this, have to sacrifice that. That revolutionaries are ordinary people, one never felt that until I met Comrade Chris.[40]

Hani also integrated this concern in the way cadres were briefed prior to being sent on missions into the country. In seeing cadres over the border he was more concerned with their 'readiness' than with the details of their mission. He did not want anyone to undertake a mission if not psychologically prepared, driven by fear of being called a coward or less revolutionary. He made them feel that there were many ways of contributing to winning the war, without entering the country. He did not want unnecessary martyrs, but that each person could 'continue fighting tomorrow'.

The life of each and every soldier used to be very important to him. He used to ask: 'Do you think there are things that are personal that you need to sort out?' His view was that if you go home with the baggage of certain personal problems that are not resolved, that are not addressed, you might not be very, very confident in fulfilling your mission – that you might *die*; and that used to concern him *very, very much*.[41]

He was aware that many had joined the army out of anger but when confronted by the actual situation of return were in fact reluctant, and believed that the army should accommodate this.

Comrade Chris managed to accommodate it because he used to deal with us individually and discuss with us and find out what troubles us, what makes us happy, you know, and that ... was very important, more important than the mission itself because these people – we have to implement these missions, and not some objects because they happen to have skills.[42]

That the ANC was seen as and acted out the role of a substitute parent also affected individual parents and their relationship with their own biological children. It appears to have resulted in specific conceptions of parental responsibility and relationships as part of this vision of a broader love of the people that tended to supplant or downgrade the interpersonal, including responsibilities towards children. Freddy Reddy, a psychiatrist working in MK camps in Angola from the 1970s, reported a consultation concerning a young man who left the country to join MK, but mainly to meet his father. He had hardly known his father, who had been in prison during his childhood and then joined MK outside. Reddy describes their meeting and the differing reactions of father and son:

The first time he saw his father was on the parade ground during inspection. He was very excited, but his father gave not the slightest sign of recognition, nor did he contact him later after the inspection. The boy was emotionally devastated. He felt that his father did not love him. It was not very long before he developed confusional psychosis. On asking his father why he ignored his son, he [the father] replied that *everyone in the camp was his* [child]: 'I could not give him special treatment.'[43]

How widespread was this attitude? To what extent was the embrace of this wider notion of parenting an adoption of wider responsibilities towards children in general, or primarily a mode for displacing or repressing the need for responsibility towards one's own children? To the extent that the organisation sought to fill that gap, as we have seen, it was only possible to do so in a partial way.

◎

This chapter has examined the ways in which joining the underground entailed a rupture in people's lives, a break in the normal pattern of relationships that would sustain them in their lives had they not taken the course involving secrecy, warfare and other stressful factors. That a rupture took place did not mean there was no longer a need for relationships and other emotional attachments that could not automatically be fulfilled in the situation of underground work. Notions such as the ANC or Communist Party as parents or family helped meet the need for parental figures. Also, the desire to fulfil oneself through interpersonal love was supplanted by 'love for the people' (which could only have served as a metaphorical substitute if it was viewed as a substitute at all).

As we have seen, there were various ways in which people tried to match and meet both political imperatives and personal needs. Though personal needs would never be entirely fulfilled in revolutionary situations, the example of Walter and Albertina Sisulu shows how a couple's relationship with their children could sometimes go beyond that of many other revolutionary parents in seeking to maintain conventional responsibilities as well as revolutionary ones. In similar vein, Chris Hani's conception of the revolution encompassed a real concern for the personal.

The subordination of the personal has also been examined in relation to the tension that exists between individual powers of judgement and the imperatives of the organisation. Having chosen to be part of an organisational arrangement in conditions of great danger, cadres were called upon or saw the need to sacrifice elements of their individual judgement or defer to that of the collective leadership of the organisation to which they owed allegiance. In the sphere of political judgements there was little doubt that the individual submission to the collective was accepted as necessary for security and other reasons.

The overall picture does appear to indicate the general suppression of 'the personal' in favour of 'the collective', but this is qualified. The social and psychological care was undoubtedly inadequate in relation to the problems encountered. But some people did not admit to their psychological difficulties, possibly because of the prevailing atmosphere of a military situation, but also resources were limited. There were psychiatrists and there were possibly other individuals besides Chris Hani who tried to take steps to consider human beings as a whole and not purely in terms of their fighting capacity. We do not know, but that there was a Chris Hani and possibly many others like him needs to be factored into our understanding, along with the presence of itinerant psychiatrists like Freddy Reddy.

8

THE RE-ESTABLISHMENT OF ANC
HEGEMONY AFTER 1976

It was never inevitable or preordained that the ANC would achieve hegemony within the liberation struggle and in the new democratic South Africa. Indeed, there were times in the history of the organisation when it was virtually dormant. In the period we have reviewed, 1950 to 1976, the ANC weathered storms so severe that some felt it could not and would not survive.

That it did survive depended in the first place on the way in which the ANC had, over decades, inserted itself into the cultural consciousness of people, becoming part of their sense of being, even if at times of great repression there was no public forum or outlet for this identity. This continuing consciousness of belonging to the ANC, or 'being ANC', was captured in an interview conducted with Joseph Faniso Mati, an organiser in Port Elizabeth in the 1950s. He remarked: 'When I asked a person to join the organisation – even if the person had no money for a membership card of the ANC – that one would say: "Oh my child, who is not a member of the ANC? We are all members of the ANC!"'[1] Even though fear may have reduced some to silence, this consciousness nevertheless remained present. Over time it was transmitted from generation to generation in a variety of ways, depending on the degree and scope of repression.

In the late 1970s, and especially in the 1980s, the political landscape of South Africa began to change substantially. Until then, the ANC's presence within the country as well as the spread of its ideas had tended to be covert; both were largely confined to exile or prison. The phase beginning after 1976 saw a growing expression, whether open or 'coded', of adherence to the ANC and its principles, primarily through other organisations because open alignment to the ANC still carried heavy penalties. Even the coded expression of support for the ideas of the ANC, given the wide definitions in the repressive legislation then, carried the potential of prosecution. But gradually a climate was created for freer expression and, despite continued repression, a space was simultaneously opened for public opposition to apartheid. Ideas and programmes intimately associated with the ANC, in particular those contained in the Freedom Charter, were advanced. Another way of manifesting this partisanship was the recognition of Nelson Mandela as a national leader to whom allegiance was pledged.

This change in conditions was primarily a result of initiatives of the anti-apartheid opposition, which forced concessions from the regime. But it also derived from attempts by the government to relieve some of the pressures under which it was forced to function, by appearing to 'normalise' the political situation. These pressures to which the regime responded included those exerted by the major Western states, and by domestic and international capital, which sought a stable investment climate.

It is a paradox that the openings for freer political expression were created during the premiership and then presidency of PW Botha, who is now generally remembered as a cantankerous old reactionary. Such spaces were intended to absorb black frustrations and direct these towards manageable political (and labour) activities, albeit not necessarily in direct support of the apartheid government. By allowing these openings to opposition forces, the regime hoped to engender an appearance of political 'normality' while nevertheless sustaining minority rule. Unfortunately for Botha, the opposition used these spaces for different and more far-reaching objectives and frustrated what his government had intended. The opening provided also led to the development of modes of opposition more threatening to the continuation of apartheid rule than ever before.

In part, the ANC underground made use of these spaces for radical purposes – often in response to mass activity which it had itself not initiated, around housing, forced removals, strikes and similar activities linking the specific grievances to the wider challenge to apartheid rule. But in many cases, a conscious, deliberate attempt was made by underground operatives to increase the scope of their public activities in the late 1970s and 1980s, enlarging the geographical area and places of operation, previously closed, where mass mobilisation could be initiated and undertaken. Zubeida Jaffer, for example, used her local community and worker networks in order to raise funds and draw on resources to sustain MK units and other illegal activities. While working as a social worker during the upsurge of the 1980s Shirley Gunn, in the pamphlets she produced underground, tried to point to the wider implications of the activities being conducted in the legal struggles. What was seen as an individual or specific grievance of an individual or a community was connected to the notion of wider oppression caused by apartheid rule. It was intended that the limited local struggles should thus be linked to the broader national struggle for liberation.[2]

The gradual establishment of ANC hegemony was a product of the combined efforts of a variety of forces, one of these being the long-term efforts and continued presence of the organised underground. In order to understand this process, it is important to spell out what is meant by hegemony in this context. Hegemony did not inhere merely in numerical superiority or in the displacement of other political bodies as the most popular element among the anti-apartheid forces. The assertion of ANC hegemony involved a number of elements, which we shall now consider. In each of these respects, the ANC and its allies differed in varying degrees from other opponents of apartheid.

What distinguished the ANC to a large degree (but not absolutely) was the amount of time it devoted to establishing structures, its modes of organising, and the scope of its activities, which extended further and wider than those of other political bodies. This had not always been the case. In fact the development of the ANC as a well-organised political body occurred relatively late in its history. It was not until the 1940s that the ANC devoted itself to much besides annual conferences.[3] Until then it seldom organised its members on a regular basis or even for campaigns. In particular it did not consider challenging the white regime, nor did it develop the strategies and tactics, or mechanisms and structures, for undertaking such a venture. Only in the 1940s were serious attempts made, by ANC President Dr Xuma and Secretary-General James Calata, to build a functioning administration and attempt to establish an organisational link between the leadership and other levels of the ANC.

Much of the emphasis on developing organisational strength came from Communist sources. According to Rusty Bernstein, when people consider Communist influence on the ANC they generally focus on ideological input, whereas in his view the Communist contribution was primarily at the level of organisation. Reflecting on the 1940s and early 1950s, Bernstein suggests:

> The work content of a Party member's day was very considerable and they were used to working as an organised group, but the ANC was not, the ANC was a very loose organisation. You could join the ANC and pay five shillings and not ever attend a branch meeting ... our people brought into the ANC and for that matter into the trade unions a very particular style of work, which wasn't indigenous to these organisations and I think that was our biggest contribution. Frankly, a lot of commentators write about the great theoretical contribution we made to these organisations. I think, in some ways, it's the other way round. They made a great theoretical contribution to us, but we made a really important organisational contribution to them and gave them what they lacked, which was a sort of organised disciplined core. The few spread out through the branches and through the various organisations, and this is what enabled them, I think, to grow as a great mass organisation.[4]

Bernstein may be correct but nevertheless underestimate the Communist ideological influence, which has been indicated earlier. Not only did this emphasis on organisation within the ANC generally develop at a relatively late phase in its history, but the consolidation of organisational structures was interrupted by both the Treason Trial, which impeded the activities of top leadership from 1956 till 1961, and the period of deep repression starting in the 1960s. The new emphasis on sustainable organisation was supposed to be a long-term, patient process whereby enduring structures would be built, irrespective of the conditions. Obviously this did not happen in every structure that was established and it would be modified depending on the existence of conditions of legality or illegality.

In the context of the ANC's banned status, this often meant slow work, the careful selection and induction of recruits, and some elapse of time between initial organising and the point when something was done or visible results were seen. What all this required was a frame of mind that did not seek 'quick fixes' and a recognition that operatives were in for the long haul. As we have seen, such an approach led to the impatience that many BC activists felt with the ANC.

During the 1970s, popular organisations emerged like the independent trade unions, residents' committees, umbrella organisations like the Soweto Committee of Ten, civics like the Port Elizabeth Black Civic Organisation (PEBCO) and the Soweto Civic Association (SCA), organisations around 'squatter' communities like those formed in Crossroads, and more generalised housing organisations like the Durban Housing Action Committee (DHAC), student organisations like the Congress of South African Students (COSAS) and Azanian Students' Organisation (AZASO),[5] and emerging women's and youth organisations in the Western Cape, Eastern Cape and Natal. Organisations were built in a variety of sectors – in communities, in the workplace, among women and youth – often with the advice and involvement of veterans, some of whom were former political prisoners.

As much attention was supposed to be placed on spreading the message as on organising a base for sustaining it. This was not always achieved, as the later UDF slogan 'From mobilisation to organisation' recognised. This slogan was meant to convey that mobilising for a campaign or a mass rally was not the same as sustaining that support base. Enduring organisation was required to develop cadres who would organise for the long term – how long the long term would be was not then known. The cadres had to be able to enjoy victories as well as survive defeats, drawing lessons from both. Despite the emphasis on organisation by the ANC and its allies, its implementation was uneven.

Thus the first step towards achieving ANC hegemony was the diffusion of what activists refer to as 'our way of working', the way the ANC organised people. Another way in which its hegemony was increasingly manifested was through symbolic identification with the ANC. This was accomplished in a number of ways. In the first place, and at some risk, activists might 'show the colours' – hold a flag with ANC colours, erect a banner, wear the colours on their clothes or put on an ANC cap, aligning themselves to the organisation's symbols in these ways. Clearly engaging in such activities still entailed considerable risk, as is evident in the conviction of individuals in numerous cases for furthering the aims of a banned organisation by displaying the colours of the ANC (even on a mug). The hoisting of ANC flags at funerals became widespread. As an indication of the complexity of the politics that evolved, the first funeral at which the ANC flag was raised may well have been that of Hennie Ferrus. Ferrus was a former Robben Islander, who on release worked in the 'collaborationist' (Coloured) Labour Party.

Identification with the ANC was also made through the multiple ways in which Nelson Mandela was projected as the legitimate leader of the people of South Africa. This was often done in the context of campaigns for his release and that of other political prisoners. While many people may have pressed for his release on purely humanitarian grounds, a substantial number saw such campaigns as also implying the necessity of ANC leadership of the country.

In the same period, the Freedom Charter and its demands began to be popularised, initially at a purely symbolic level, while later its ideological implications came increasingly to the fore in debate. Even without any ideological content, the Freedom Charter was a powerful symbolic way of identifying with the ANC. Clauses of the Charter became household words, through being heard or seen or chanted. Without having studied the Charter, many people would know by heart certain passages or phrases, especially 'The People Shall Govern!' and 'The People Shall Share in the Country's Wealth!' Such phrases were also painted on walls or displayed on banners at demonstrations.

Underlying much of this symbolism, and in fact embraced in such slogans as 'ANC is the nation', was an attempt to identify the ANC symbolically with the future of the country and the ANC as the authentic representative of the people of South Africa. This equation of a liberation movement with the nation was part of the contestation that had arisen against minority rule in South Africa and elsewhere. While it had a positive unifying element, it also carried latent dangers that later emerged to some extent in South Africa – the distrust of pluralism and a failure to recognise adequately the range of identities that constitute the human components as well as the distinct interests within 'the nation'.[6]

A third manifestation of the ANC's increasing hegemony was the popular acceptance of MK both as an army and as a symbol of a whole people resisting, fighting and piercing the apparently invincible defences of apartheid. It contributed to ANC hegemony at a powerful symbolic level, quite independent of its actual military capacity and the threat it may have posed to the security of the apartheid state. That soldiers of a people who had been denied military training by the apartheid regime took up arms and attacked the apartheid security forces carried important symbolic power.

Thus an attack on a police station, whatever its status in regard to the overall balance of military forces, filled people with great emotion. In any earlier period such an idea would have been inconceivable. The ability of soldiers from MK to deal a blow to the symbols and agents of apartheid was something new. Such military activity was seen as growing out of a popular power, and filled people with pride and awe.

MK, as the ANC declared, was 'born of the people'. Whatever its military power may have been, it was an army that arose from a source entirely outside the white regime. It emerged after an uncertain beginning into formations that were able to attack major apartheid targets, such as Sasol oil refinery and Voortrekkerhoogte military headquarters. MK was seen as representing the 'sons and daughters of our soil', as Radio Freedom would express it, and it carried enormous popular expectations – expectations that MK could not in fact realise. Nevertheless, the glimpses of MK's strength gave power to people's emotions and empowered resistance on other fronts as well.

The achievement of ANC hegemony was not a smooth and straightforward process leading to the simple adoption of its principles, strategies and tactics. Throughout the 1970s and 1980s its position was contested by other political groups and traditions. Even though these were surmounted by the ANC or came to enjoy less support, they did leave an impact on the ANC. In the Western Cape, for example, the local Unity Movement, though small in actual terms, influenced those in ANC-aligned organisations. Even today one can detect a Unity Movement inflection in much of the Western Cape ANC discourse. More significant was the influence of Black Consciousness on the ANC. It is important that we do not assess the significance of BC purely by its current electoral strength. The BC people who joined the ANC left a mark on the latter, changing aspects of its thinking and strengthening certain currents within it. Moreover, we need to question the tendency to see BC as an immature political manifestation, which people left behind them in a process of political maturation to join the ANC. This has been the way in which many former BC adherents depict and understand their political evolution, but it is not an accurate reflection of the significance of Black Consciousness as a political tradition in South Africa.

Not only was the ANC position mediated by the impact of recruits from other traditions. Even within broad anti-apartheid ranks there were various ideological divisions and contests. One of the most important, especially in the 1980s in the trade union movement, was that between 'workerists' and 'populists/nationalists', reflecting divisions between those who emphasised the class character of the struggle and those who emphasised national oppression or sought to combine both. Then again, in particular sites of struggle, issues would arise which on occasion would be resolved by the adoption of a 'Congress position', even by groups or traditions outside the ANC. In the context of struggles around education, for example, the Congress position of nonracialism was gradually adopted by the previously BC-aligned AZASO (the Azanian Students' Organisation).

An issue might sometimes have arisen in the context of a community struggle, where the question may have been whether workers should only involve themselves in issues at the workplace or support what was being undertaken in the place where they lived or by their own children. Alternatively, on the community side, support may have been called for an activity outside the immediate community, a workers' strike in particular, though it was often likely that members of the community were part of the workforce concerned. The degree to which this might have been understood as part of the national struggle may have varied.

What then were the main political ideas underpinning ANC hegemony which differentiated it from other traditions? The basic ideas which came to characterise the Congress position were broadly those of the Freedom Charter, encapsulated especially in the first paragraph, which declared: 'South Africa belongs to all who live in it, black and white.' This declaration diverged sharply from the position of both the Africanist and BC organisations.[7]

The Charter covered a broad range of concerns and related to a variety of issues that touched directly on people's lives, and perhaps for this reason could win the adherence of a wide range of supporters. But this is not to say that the Charter itself had a single meaning or was unproblematic, uncontroversial and uncontested. Depending on the interests and inclinations of its adherents, certain clauses received prominence or emphasis at various times or in various contexts. Thus those concerned to counter criticism from the left tried to deflect it by emphasising the more working-class or socialist-oriented sections of the Charter. Alternatively, those who wanted to lay stress on the national character of the struggle would emphasise the type of nation envisaged by the Charter as a whole. There were many permutations, mediated in many ways by the concrete situations and type of opposition that people encountered.

Even when a position was universally accepted, its implications in practical terms were not always fully understood or not easily translated into practice. To take nonracialism, a cardinal principle of the ANC and its allies: the adoption of this principle in a situation where Africans did not work with whites might mean something quite different from one where whites and blacks met and worked together. Even where in the latter case nonracialism was adopted as a principle, this did not resolve the tensions and resentments that arose, for example, because of the privileged access and background of white and often other non-African colleagues. In the early trade union movement, white officials exercised a disproportionate influence because of their skills or connections, knowledge or experience. White officials knew whom to go to when a lawyer was required or a tax issue arose. Their own experience, in a world that was relatively new to the African unionists and the broader activists, created situations where white knowledge was a necessary resource. This was needed but it was also a cause of resentment.[8]

Similar tensions were present in popular organisations, where resources and connections were disproportionately available to whites and other minority groups who were more likely to have cars and tended to have access to funds that could be used to embark on specific ventures. This, as indicated in Chapter 5, sometimes led to relationships of patronage, where control of funds enabled some to influence the political orientation of people to whom they provided resources for specific activities.

Another major defining feature of the Congress position, indeed its overall strategic orientation, was the emphasis on national liberation. This meant assembling a combination of people and forces from a range of sectors and communities who in varying ways felt the impact of apartheid oppression. What emerged was a cross-class and cross-community alliance, involving also a small number of progressive whites.

At various moments, the emphasis on the national democratic struggle or the national question came under attack from segments of the left and led, especially in the 1970s and 1980s, to much discussion of the relationship between national liberation and socialism. While an emphasis remained on national liberation at the same time as a large degree of support for socialism emerged within the social base of the Congress forces, the exact relationship between the two was constantly reformulated and debated.

Socialism was very much in vogue during this period. Paradoxically the word 'socialism' is seldom heard in polite ANC circles today, except to laugh at the foibles of 'our youthful fantasies'. At the same time, the ANC and the government in defending conservative economic policies like GEAR sometimes deploy the discourse of Marxism and Leninism.[9]

A third defining feature of the Congress position was its self-representation as part of a democratic movement. In contrast to the apartheid regime imposing its policies from above, the ANC was depicted as arising from below and involved in a struggle for democracy in which, according to the words of the Freedom Charter, 'the people shall govern'. The exact content of this democracy underwent various permutations over time. In this way the meanings attached to democracy in the popular power period, with substantial development of grassroots organisational activity in street committees and similar bodies during the 1980s, constituted a substantial reinterpretation of previous notions of democracy and the application of the Freedom Charter provisions in novel ways.

Like any political movement, the ANC and its allies continually confronted a tension between the democracy it was advocating for the society as a whole and the creation of democracy within itself. Obviously the overall situation where the ANC and the advocacy of its policies were illegal was not conducive to openness and free debate. Though a popular insurrection was in progress, this did not mean that people felt free to confide their beliefs to other comrades, especially if betrayal could lead to arrest. Even where desired by members, conventional democratic practices could not be safely or easily sustained.

This kind of situation lent itself to forms of decision-making where small caucuses made initial decisions, which were then sold to wider bodies. Especially where some leaders were under forms of legal restriction, the implementation of decisions was sometimes engineered in ways that led to complaints of undemocratic practices. As for the ANC underground, which was often a crucial reference point during the era of struggle, by definition it operated by 'remote influence' or 'remote control', with orders coming from 'faceless individuals'. Even in above-ground organisations like trade unions, delays in discussion often arose for apparently inexplicable reasons that seem to have been due to the need for consultation, locally and abroad, with veterans from SACTU and other ANC allies. Obviously the overall situation, in which the ANC was illegal and the advocacy of its policies was illegal, created a framework unconducive to openness and the type of debate that could be engaged in where there was no fear of repression.

A final key feature of Congress politics was that it was intended to be mass-driven. 'The people' would drive the process and articulate their own demands through their own structures, which they had built on various fronts. For many years this outcome had been envisaged by the ANC, though its exact manifestation could not be clearly imagined. The ANC had for some time wanted to operate in the public terrain, not only through the presence of leading individuals, but through the masses making their strength felt on a number of fronts. This intention may account for the ANC spending some time in wooing Chief MG Buthelezi and his Inkatha movement before finally deciding that his agenda was not the same as theirs. When popular resistance began to gather force in the late 1970s, various forces were linked under the influence of the ANC programme to the conception of a struggle that was national – one, that is, whose scope was meant to cover the entire country and all its peoples. Consequently, the reach of popular organisations allied to the ANC opened up areas which had not previously been penetrated and sectors that had not previously fallen under its sway, sometimes bringing a range of contradictions, as with the establishment of organisations like the Congress of Traditional Leaders of South Africa (CONTRALESA).

◎

The achievements of the ANC after embarking on armed struggle cannot be attributed to any one factor or force alone. Nor indeed can the establishment of ANC hegemony be seen as emanating purely from formal ANC activities or directives alone. Rather, that hegemony arose from activities of a variety of forces, formally and informally connected to the ANC or allied bodies. The main actors were the underground operatives, the political prisoners on Robben Island, the movement in exile, MK, and the decisive entry of popular forces from the late 1970s. We shall examine the contribution of each in turn.

The underground was a key factor that kept the ANC alive during the period when it was illegal in South Africa. It helped widen its base of support and prepared a group of cadres for opening up legal space in which opposition to apartheid could be conducted. Like the older comrades on Robben Island and in exile, the underground operatives were the bearers of a historical tradition that was communicated to younger people. In that sense the underground formed part of a continuing, enduring cultural presence which survived the darkest periods of repression. In communicating this heritage and the lessons of this history, they helped equip a new generation for the struggles of the late 1970s and 1980s, providing the tools that enabled what had previously been forced underground to emerge increasingly above ground, despite the legal sanctions barring this.

As a result the generation that grew up in the late 1970s and 1980s had a greater sense of the history of the struggle. Often this understanding may have lacked complexity, but through the presence of the underground a concept of what it meant to be part of 'Congress' became diffused amongst the new generation. This politicised their activities in a manner that transformed them into political action with a clear Congress orientation. At the same time this new generation, as with all previous ones, brought its own ideas that did not derive from previous examples but made its own impact and influenced interpretations of traditions and practice in a novel way.

The ANC was in many respects an enduring cultural presence in South Africa, even during the darkest periods. This is perfectly compatible with the contention of many writers that the 1960s saw an atmosphere of fear and demoralisation, so that many supporters of the ANC kept their attachment secret except amongst trusted friends. Nevertheless, an ANC presence persisted in varying ways in both urban and rural areas, in memories, allusions and songs. Even apparent silence might mean a stealthy but carefully planned support. At the same time, we should remember that the basis for ANC support cannot be measured through membership figures or public activity in the name of the organisation. Even in its earlier legal period, we have noted, there were many people who considered themselves to be 'ANC' without ever joining. Dr James Moroka was not himself a member of the ANC when elected President at the decisive 1949 Congress when the organisation adopted a programme of action.[10]

Another key force in securing ANC hegemony was Robben Island. Together with other prisons, though to a much larger extent, Robben Island played a crucial role in winning over people who were not members of the ANC on entering jail and in general consolidating ANC support among people who would later re-enter South African society in various sectors – trade unions, political bodies, civics and other community structures.

As prisoners were located in various parts of the jail, depending on their perceived seniority in the ANC (though some who were not in the top leadership were placed in the same section as Mandela, Sisulu and Mbeki), there were difficulties in communication. Various position papers were written and then smuggled by elaborate means to all members, who read and discussed them. Each section of the prison conducted its own *umrabulo* (political discussions) and held formal courses of study of ANC history as well as Marxism. While Marxism was taught, the Communist Party did not formally operate as an organisation independent of the ANC on the island.

In cases of dispute about policy or principles, the issues were sometimes resolved on a hierarchical basis. For instance, where conflict over an interpretation raged for some time, it was usually referred to the top leadership for a decision, though they were not always in agreement. In particular, disputes continued between Govan Mbeki (allied with Harry Gwala) and Raymond Mhlaba on the one side, and Mandela and Sisulu on the other, about the extent to which the struggle for socialism should be incorporated in the vision of the ANC, something Mandela and Sisulu resisted. Besides the ideological component, the dispute was partly a contest of Mandela's leadership.

Over the years extensive political education courses were developed on the island. These inducted new members into the ideas and practices of the ANC and consolidated the understanding of others. As a result some prisoners like Mosiuoa 'Terror' Lekota, currently Minister of Defence, crossed from BC to ANC because of continual exposure to the ideas of the ANC leadership. Robben Island was a place where people became intellectuals in the sense in which Gramsci used the term – inasmuch as their practice (irrespective of their academic qualifications) entailed an intellectual role. Significantly, some of the most important teachers on the island, men like Elias Motsoaledi and Sisulu, were not conventionally trained but mainly self-taught intellectuals.

The third force in the achievement of ANC hegemony was exile. The 1976 uprising led to many young activists getting out of the country, partly because they were on the run from police and could not continue their education inside the country, partly in order to find a way of returning, equipped to meet the apartheid forces by military means. Many of these people had only a vague idea of the difference between ANC and PAC or of the level and form of organisation that existed outside. Though neither the ANC nor PAC was initially equipped to deal with this influx, the ANC gradually developed a greater capacity to house those who joined it, and also to give them training in its political ideas.[11] Most recruits were offered a choice between education and military training. While the ANC itself favoured the former, many young people insisted on going to the military camps.

From an early stage of their admission, some form of political education took place. Many of the youth resisted the idea of nonracialism and in some cases objected to lectures by white comrades. Others, perhaps the majority, were not interested in completing or extending their education; they wanted to return to South Africa gun in hand and take on the apartheid regime. It required a great deal of explanation to convince them that the ANC army was not a conventional one, but a political army. As was repeatedly said, what mattered most was not that someone held a gun, but who was behind the gun and what their understanding was.[12]

From the early days of their reception in neighbouring southern African states and in camps overseas, the ideas of the ANC were instilled in these young men and women. Many of them, like the late 'Comrade Mzala' (Jabulani Nxumalo),[13] became intellectuals and trainers in their own right, contributing to the political doctrines of the ANC or enriching it from their experiences of other traditions like Black Consciousness.[14] This enrichment cannot be measured purely in terms of the absorption of political ideas but also as the sense of psychological emancipation that these youth brought into the ANC.

Once again, the character of the ANC's position was contested within the exile community and passed through various changes. At the time of the ANC's banning in 1960, Marxist ideas were present in the thinking of many leading figures who had joined the ANC, but this was an individual choice rather than an organisational orientation. Over the years and decades that followed, a marked ideological shift took place and the overall orientation of the ANC came to be heavily influenced by Marxist thought. This was also evident in the foreign policy of the ANC, which became closely aligned to that of the USSR and its allies.[15]

This orientation was reflected from an early stage in the literature used for the induction of new recruits. While the ANC history, strategies and tactics were central elements in its teachings, Marxist education also became a key part of what was taught in the camps and in other classes, as the published lectures of Jack Simons confirm.[16] This education was often empowering. Totsie Memela mentioned in an interview that having come from a poor background, on being taught Marxist beliefs she felt proud for the first time to have come from the working class.[17]

Over the years this dominant orientation of the ANC in exile came to ground the interpretations of ANC policies, strategies and tactics. It also helped popularise socialism within the ANC in the late 1970s and 1980s. This is not to say that there were no serious differences within the overall orientation. Distinct factions with somewhat different visions emerged that were associated with underground groups operating independently of each other within the country. The units to which the late David Rabkin, Sue Rabkin and Jeremy Cronin belonged in Cape Town, like myself in Durban, were linked to Joe Slovo and Ronnie Kasrils; in Natal units clustered round Pravin Gordhan were primarily connected to Mac Maharaj; others again were related to Thabo Mbeki or Jacob Zuma and so on. The figures in exile, I later discovered, differed sharply over strategy and tactics (see Chapter 5 above). Naturally this impacted on those to whom they related inside the country.

Nevertheless, whatever divergences may have existed in interpretation, the external wing built a cohesive ANC orientation which became a reference point for people inside the country, especially through Radio Freedom and journals like the *African Communist*, *Sechaba* and *Mayibuye*. The importance of the exile influence was that it transmitted ANC beliefs in an overall package, emphasising that 'the main content of the present stage of the South African revolution is the national liberation of the largest and most oppressed group – the African people.'[18] And within this broad mass of African people who had to be mobilised, special emphasis was placed on the role of the working class. Simultaneously emphasis was placed on the nonracial character of the struggle aiming to liberate all and inviting the participation of members of all groups including progressive whites. The objective was to implement the vision of the Freedom Charter, which represented a manifestation of the goals of the National Democratic Revolution. This did not mean only political liberation but also the transformation of the overall conditions of oppression and exploitation. This theme was of course open to more than one interpretation.

In a practical sense this section cannot be ended without noting the importance of the ANC's interventions from its headquarters in Lusaka and the strategic directions it gave, in joining internal and external forces. In a sense, the ANC succeeded in that it propounded a vision that was more coherent than that of other organisations and whose understanding corresponded more closely to what people believed was necessary or seemed possible. The ANC's National Executive Committee understood, sometimes better than the UDF in the 1980s, the language of the various constituencies, language that would persuade them to undertake certain tasks. When, for example, the UDF struggled to persuade students to return to school, they responded (albeit temporarily) to the ANC's call to return when it asserted that the 'schools are your trenches'. Militaristic this may have been, but it struck a chord. This was an important feature of the success of the ANC's strategic vision in mobilising and organising people from a variety of sectors and regions.

The last force we need to take account of in explaining the ANC's hegemony was MK. MK's actual military power was not what was attributed to it by many activists. But its very presence, the existence of a military arm of the ANC which attacked apartheid targets, was an important element in establishing ANC hegemony over the anti-apartheid forces in general. It was in the period immediately after 1976 when MK first fired shots on South African soil. This captured the popular imagination. Interviewees testify in the early 1960s to the psychological impact of seeing black people carrying arms and, in some cases, seeing Mandela in military uniform.[19]

Although one cannot claim that MK had the capacity to overthrow the apartheid regime, there is little doubt that many people cherished this hope, that MK inspired them greatly, and that its existence and the military achievements that it did secure were an important element in ANC hegemony being consolidated. People often did not judge an attack, say on a police station, in terms of the overall balance of military power, and tended to overrate its significance, but military forays of this kind were important in the perception of the ANC as the force that would bring freedom.

◎

This chapter is by way of an epilogue. The earlier part of this book set out to 'render visible' a relatively unacknowledged part of South Africa's resistance history and to extract its various meanings, meanings that go well beyond purely organisational questions. As we have seen, these relate to distinct identities, questions of gender relations, relationships between the personal and the liberation movement collective, and modes of organisation specific to conspiratorial small groups.

The way in which conventional scholarship treats knowledge is that the written word stands higher in the hierarchy of knowledge than what may be known by many who cannot write. Before these insights can form part of what is called knowledge it needs to be changed into the literate form. Much of this book has dealt with that body of knowledge or knowledges that are marginalised because they have not been recorded in written form. It has also sought to make visible a range of activities that have not found a place or adequate place in the existing literature, partly because they were not recorded in documents. It started in a phase prior to the ANC's banning in 1960 because what was done in the early ANC attempts to prepare for underground continued to have a bearing on subsequent organisational efforts in the post-Rivonia period, indeed right up until the 1980s. Likewise the successful reconstitution of the South African Communist Party as an underground organisation had a continuing impact beyond the SACP itself. The experience of the Communists had considerable influence on the early underground activities of the ANC and the re-establishment of the ANC underground.

It may be that this book makes a contribution towards rethinking the periodisation of ANC history in so far as it shows the differences between various decades and forms of struggle as not being as stark and sharp as most works have done. It shows that there was substantial continuity within ruptures, ruptures within continuities, and blurring of periods, with habits of a future phase manifested in embryonic form before the actual onset of the new phase, just as practices of a period supposedly over tend often to continue into 'new periods'.

The book breaks from the approach which treats exile and internal activity as inevitably separate political experiences. This is not to suggest that every exile experience was part of the underground. But as we have shown, in many cases the training and preparations from outside were integrally connected to what people were able to carry out within South Africa. Even for those who never left the country or had any contact with externally based individuals, the reach of the ANC and its media like Radio Freedom was often a major influence on their activities and ideas and on the development of ANC hegemony.

The book steps back from a historical account and tries to dissect underground organisation in South Africa as a particular type of social and political phenomenon, operating according to distinct rules that are in many ways unique. In certain respects this has to do with the ways an underground unit must operate in order to avoid detection and perform its work – qualities that in some ways are completely different from modes of politics practised in normal times.

In addition to unpacking these 'rules' and modes of operation, this study has brought to the surface the gendered nature of underground organisation. Men and women entered into activities that in the case of MK were essentially militarised and traditionally the preserve of men. As we have seen, the character of gender relations within the ANC underground cannot be simply categorised. In entering male-dominated structures, in particular the army, women often encountered difficulties in fulfilling themselves and realising their capacities or even using the training they had received to the full. But partly because of their own assertiveness and partly because of the specific commitment of some leading individuals like Chris Hani, the tendency to marginalise and sometimes abuse women was combated.

This study has also looked at the tendency of revolutionary struggles to subsume individual judgements and personal needs within the collective. There are a variety of ways in which a revolution tends to 'take over' the individual and sideline his or her personal judgement or needs. As with the earlier chapter on gender, the study has uncovered countervailing tendencies.

In all, underground activity contributed to the opening of a new phase where the ANC moved from rebuilding its organisation and defensive action towards an offensive on a wide range of fronts. The creation of these new conditions cannot be credited to any one element. It was the total impact of the various forces ranged against the regime (including international diplomatic and solidarity activities, not discussed here) which led to a situation where negotiations between the apartheid government and the ANC first emerged as an option.

In the period that followed, the apartheid regime was not able to maintain its control and sustain its governance. At the same time, the forces of opposition, despite their increased range and effectiveness, were not of sufficient power to defeat the apartheid government completely. This is the state of what Gramsci calls 'reciprocal siege',[20] where negotiations become an option and the contending parties are forced to reach a settlement. It is sufficient to note that the underground organisation of the ANC was an important element in bringing this about.

Gail Gerhart writes:

[After the defeats of the mid-1960s] hard questions faced the decimated opposition. How could blacks regroup and resist a white regime that was intransigent, powerfully armed, and bolstered by the major western powers? Could the liberation movements from exile effect major change through a strategy of guerrilla warfare, or would change depend principally on internal political resistance?[21]

Contrary to the dichotomy Gerhart proposes, I hope this book has shown that the assumption of a choice between externally initiated guerrilla warfare and internal political resistance does not correspond to the way in which resistance politics were played out. Moreover, the notion of the 'liberation movements from exile' or the phrase 'the exiled ANC' in regular use seems to imply that the ANC's existence was tied to its structures outside the country.[22] As we have seen, this is not true, especially if we decline a definition of the ANC which is restricted to formal card-carrying members, illegal within the country after 1960. Finally, while the authors may pose a choice between guerrilla activity and political resistance, the one allegedly being externally initiated and the other being internal, was it necessary to choose? Or was the necessity rather to find a formula for combining these? To the extent that these were combined, especially in the period after 1976, the danger for the apartheid regime escalated.

In fact, the process of establishing ANC hegemony within the country is the story of the combination of internal and external, of the merging of efforts through a variety of formal and informal organisational methods over a long period.

LIST OF INTERVIEWS

'A', 3 August, 2004, Umtata (anonymity requested)

'B', 14 January 2000, Stockholm (anonymity requested)

Shun Balton, 4 August 2003, Johannesburg

Brian Bunting, 18 February 2003, Cape Town

Linus Dlamini, 13 May, 15 July, 17 August, 2005, Pretoria

Noloyiso Gasa, 23 December 2002, Johannesburg

Pravin Gordhan, 13 April 2003, Pretoria

Shirley Gunn, 26 January, 28 February 2005, Cape Town

Chris Hani, 10 February 1992, Johannesburg

Zubeida Jaffer, 25 January, 2005, Cape Town

Pallo Jordan, 20 February 2003, Cape Town

Ahmed Kathrada, 18 February 2003, Cape Town

Amos Lengisi, 14 September 2005, Elliot

Makgothi, Henry, 3 March 2003, Johannesburg.

B (Malume) Manci, 29 March 2003, Johannesburg

Mzwandile Mandubu, 29 July 2004, East London

Ike Maphotho, 28 January 2004, Polokwane

Paul Mashatile, 22 April 2003, Johannesburg

Petros 'Shoes' Mashigo, 27 October 2003, Pretoria

Amos Masondo, 10 March 2003, Johannesburg

Stan Mathabatha, 30 January 2004, Polokwane

Joe Matthews, 20 February 2003, Cape Town

Baleka Mbete, 19 February 2003, Cape Town

Totsie Memela-Khambule, 20 August 2003, Pretoria

Ralph Mgijima, 15 July 2003, Johannesburg

AN Mhlebi, 3 August 2004, Umtata

Sobizana Mngqikana, 2 February 2001, Stockholm

Victor Moche, 23 July 2002, Johannesburg

France Mohlala, 29 January 2004, Polokwane

Keith Mokoape, 22 August 2003, Pretoria

Murphy Morobe, 26 August 2003, Midrand

Pharephare Mothupi, 28 January 2004, Polokwane

Radilori John Moumakwa, 15 May 2003, Mafikeng

Eric Mtshali, 8 February 2003, Johannesburg

Dipuo Mvelase, 29 June 1993, Johannesburg

Prema Naidoo, 12 March 2003, Johannesburg

Billy Nair, 1 February 2003, Cape Town

Cleopas Ndlovu, 30 June 2003, Durban

Matthews Ngcobo, 12 October 2005, Johannesburg

Steward Ngwenya, 4 December 2002, Johannesburg

John Nkadimeng, January 2003, Johannesburg

Zingiva Nkondo, 18 September, 2002, Johannesburg

John Pampallis, 5 August 2002, Johannesburg

N Barney Pityana, 9 August 2003, Pretoria

Robbie Potenza, 13 May 2003, Johannesburg

Anton Qaba, 2 March 2004, Pietermaritzburg

Faith Radebe, 11 October 2004, Johannesburg

Nomphumelelo Setsubi, 20 August 2004, Pretoria

Nat Serache, 31 August 2002, Johannesburg

Solly Shoke, 20 September 2003, Johannesburg

Walter Sisulu, 14 September 1992, Johannesburg

Terrence Tryon, 18 August 2003, Johannesburg

Phumla Tshabalala, 13 July 2003, Johannesburg

Willie Williams, 15 April 2005, Pretoria

Interview conducted by others

Interview with Raymond Mhlaba, conducted by Phil Bonner and Barbara Harmel, Standard House, Port Elizabeth, 27, 28 October 1993

NOTES

CHAPTER 1

1   I am indebted to Professor Irina Filatova for this approach, which is elaborated on later in this chapter.

2   It is not thoroughly canvassed, however; and study of initiation (though still limited) is more substantial than that of access to spiritual healers, which has periodically emerged in interviews but has not been explored here. This is because adequate evaluation of both areas, in particular the latter, requires expertise that cannot be acquired in the period that was available for this research.

3   See, for example, TO Ranger, *Revolt in Southern Rhodesia 1896–7* (London, 1967); D Lan, *Guns and Rain: Guerrillas and Spirit Mediums in Zimbabwe* (London, Harare, 1985); N Bhebe and T Ranger (eds), *Soldiers in Zimbabwe's Liberation War* (Portsmouth NH, Harare, London, 1995); and N Bhebe and T Ranger (eds), *Society in Zimbabwe's Liberation War* (Portsmouth NH, Harare, London, 1996).

4   A valuable exception is the contemporaneous study of the South African Democratic Education Trust (SADET), which has led to the publication of two volumes of *The Road to Democracy*. They provide a wealth of new data that adds to the case against 'denialism' of underground activity. See SADET, *The Road to Democracy in South Africa*, vol 1: 1960–1970 (Cape Town, 2004) and vol 2: 1970–1980 (Pretoria, 2006).

5   T Karis and GM Gerhart (eds), *From Protest to Challenge: A Documentary History of African Politics in South Africa 1882–1990*, vol 5: *Nadir and Resurgence 1964–1979* (Pretoria, 1997), 181, 182, 279 and 280 also indicate limited presence of underground units in the period immediately before the 1976 uprising.

6   There are in fact disincentives facing scholars at universities who may want to research in the rural areas. Gone are the days when anthropologists lived for years or months in rural villages. Nowadays academics have an allowance of around R100 for telephone calls each month. After that is spent they pay out of their own pockets. Anyone wishing to arrange research interviews or accommodation or other matters in the rural areas

might well use that amount in telephone calls on one day. The incentive then for city-based academics is to do research around the cities instead.

7 Telephone conversation, 10.8.2003.

8 See J Allman (ed), *Fashioning Africa: Politics and the Power of Dress* (Indiana, 2004), Introduction.

9 Many former MK soldiers will not be interviewed before seeking permission from their commander of the time. As a reflection on hierarchies in general, it was explicitly stated by the ANC provincial secretary in Limpopo that, although I am no longer in the formal leadership, he still regarded me as his leader (interview, C Mathale, 24.1.2004). In his words: 'But now we were taught that in the ANC you don't need to occupy an office to be a leader. What you do determines your leadership. Like now, I mean, as we sit here with you, Comrade Suttner, I would regard you as my leader despite the fact that you don't occupy a specific office, but I know when I came in to become active I found you there and that itself makes you to be part of the leadership that one will always look up to. That is what we were taught.'

10 The period prior to and during imprisonment is described in R Suttner, *Inside Apartheid's Prison* (Melbourne, New York, Pietermaritzburg, 2001).

11 R Suttner, *The Freedom Charter: The People's Charter in the Nineteen-Eighties* (Cape Town, 1984).

12 Under apartheid laws, the Minister of Justice had powers to restrict movements and political activities, to banish people to various areas, and in numerous other ways curtail their political movement.

13 Operation Vula, under the command of the ANC leader Oliver Tambo and SACP leader Joe Slovo, represented a qualitatively more advanced attempt to link internal and external leadership with a view to taking underground work to a higher level. In this context, the NEC members Mac Maharaj and Ronnie Kasrils were among those who entered the country in the mid- to late 1980s. Some people (like Janet Love) worked underground in this operation for three to four years without being detected. The character of the advance that Vula represented was manifested for me by the appearance of the ANC January 8 anniversary statement on my doorstep, next to the morning newspaper. See P O'Malley, *Shades of Difference: Mac Maharaj and the Struggle for South Africa* (New York, 2007).

CHAPTER 2

1 RA Simons, *All My Life and All My Strength*. Ed R Suttner. (Johannesburg, 2004), 44–6.

2 I Filatova, 'Indoctrination or Scholarship? Education of Africans at the Communist University of the Toilers of the East in the Soviet Union 1923–1937', *Paedogogical Historica: International Journal of the History of Education* 35,1 (1999), 54–5; A Davidson, I Filatova, V Gorodnov and S

Johns (eds), *The Communist International and South Africa: Documentary History 1919–1939*, vol 1 (London, 2003), 6. The Comintern was a worldwide organisation of Communist parties, located in Moscow from 1919 until its dissolution in 1943. During its existence every Communist party was described as a 'section' of Comintern. Sometimes the Comintern intervened in the affairs of Communist parties of various countries, including that of South Africa.

3   Ibid, 6.

4   Ibid, 8ff and Simons give examples of such activity.

5   GM Gerhart, *Black Power in South Africa: The Evolution of an Ideology* (Berkeley CA, London, 1978), 131–2; T Karis and GM Gerhart (eds), *From Protest to Challenge: A Documentary History of African Politics in South Africa 1882–1964*, vol 3: *Challenge and Violence 1953–1964* (Stanford CA, 1977), 36.

6   E-mail from Gail Gerhart, 17.12.2002. This claim was met with great scepticism from Joe Matthews (interview).

7   The phrase 'Congress movement' refers to organisations allied to the ANC that were usually congresses of various types in the 1950s but comprised a wider range of organisations in the late 1970s and 1980s.

8   Karis and Gerhart (eds), vol 3, 38–9; N Mandela, *The Struggle Is My Life* (London, 1990), 40; N Mandela, *Long Walk to Freedom: The Autobiography of Nelson Mandela* (Johannesburg, 1994), 134ff.

9   Karis and Gerhart (eds), vol 3, 35–6. Capitalisation in the original.

10   Interview, J Matthews.

11   Raymond Mhlaba's interviews with Phil Bonner and Barbara Harmel suggest that the Eastern Cape proposed the plan. But the interview is unclear on whether or not it was already in operation prior to approval – this could be one reading of the transcript, which unfortunately has many gaps.

12   Mandela, *Long Walk*, 134.

13   Ibid.

14   Karis and Gerhart (eds), vol 3, 39.

15   Mandela, *Long Walk*, 136.

16   W Sisulu, *I Will Go Singing: Walter Sisulu Speaks of His Life and the Struggle for Freedom in South Africa*. In conversation with GM Houser and H Shore. (New York, nd, c 2001), 80.

17   E Sisulu, *Walter and Albertina Sisulu: In Our Lifetime* (Cape Town, 2002), 121, quoting Ministry of Justice files.

18   Ibid, 121.

19   Mandela, *Long Walk*, 134–5: A Sampson, *Mandela: The Authorised Biography* (London, 1999), 81; E Feit, *African Opposition in South Africa: The Failure of Passive Resistance* (Stanford CA, 1967), 72–5.

20   V Shubin, *ANC: A View from Moscow* (Cape Town, 1999), 11.

21   Mandela, *The Struggle*, 40, 134ff; Karis and Gerhart (eds), vol 3, 35ff; T

Lodge, *Black Politics in South Africa since 1945* (Johannesburg, 1983), 75–6; W Sisulu, *I will Go Singing*, 80–1.

22 Ibid, 79. IsiXhosa translation corrected with assistance of Nomboniso Gasa, capitalisation in original.

23 Mandela, *Long Walk*, 146: P Delius, *A Lion Amongst the Cattle* (Johannesburg, Oxford, 1996), 131ff; B Magubane, P Bonner, J Sithole, P Delius, J Cherry, P Gibbs and T April, 'The Turn to Armed Struggle' in SADET, *Road to Democracy*, vol 1, 53ff.

24 N Joseph, *Uniforms and Non-uniforms: Communication Through Clothing* (New York, Westport, London, 1986), 1.

25 See M Bose, *The Lost Hero: A Biography of Subhas Bose* (Uttar Pradesh, 2004), 207.

26 T Karis (ed), *From Protest to Challenge: A Documentary History of African Politics in South Africa 1882–1964*, vol 2: *Hope and Challenge 1935–1952* (Stanford CA, 1973), 418.

27 Mandela, *Long Walk*, 134.

28 In JK Coetzee, L Gilfillan and O Hulec (eds), *Fallen Walls: Voices from the Cells that Held Mandela and Havel* (Cape Town, 2002), 60. Emphasis added.

29 Mandela, *The Struggle*, 40.

30 Mandela, *Long Walk*, 135. See also Feit, *African Opposition* 72–3.

31 T Orie, 'Raymond Mhlaba and the Genesis of the Congress Alliance: A Political Biography' (unpublished MA thesis, University of Cape Town, 1993), 102–3.

32 'Steward' in *Shorter Oxford English Dictionary*, 1986; personal communication, Professor G Cuthbertson, 31.1.2003; interview, J Matthews; E Webster, 'Introduction' in SM Pityana and M Orkin (eds), *Beyond the Factory Floor: A Survey of COSATU Shop-Stewards* (Johannesburg, 1992), 7.

33 See A Odendaal, *Vukani Bantu!: The Beginnings of Black Protest Politics in South Africa to 1912* (Cape Town, Johannesburg, 1984), Chapters 1 and 4; P Walshe, *The Rise of African Nationalism in South Africa: The African National Congress 1912–1952* (London, 1970), Chapter 1.

34 Interview, J Matthews. That this was used later is borne out by the evidence in the SADET volumes and certain interviews that follow.

35 Mandela, *Long Walk*, 135; Anon, 'Internal Education in the Congress Alliance', *Africa Perspective* 24 (1984), 99–111; D Everatt, 'The Politics of Nonracialism: White Opposition to Apartheid 1945–1960' (unpublished DPhil thesis, Oxford University, 1990); interviews, B Nair and E Mtshali.

36 Mandela, *Long Walk*, 135.

37 Interviews, E Mtshali, C Ndlovu and L Dlamini.

38 Mandela, *Long Walk*, 135.

39 Quoted in P Bonner and L Segal, *Soweto: A History* (Cape Town, 1998), 50.

40 A Gramsci, *Selections from the Prison Notebooks*. Ed Q Hoare and G Nowell Smith. (London, 1971), 3–23.

41 Interview, Willie Williams.

42 Interviews, C Ndlovu and E Mtshali; R Suttner, 'The Formation and Functioning of Intellectuals Within the ANC-Led Liberation Movement' in T Mkandawire (ed), *African Intellectuals* (Dakar, London, 2005).

43 Anon, 'Internal Education'; interviews, E Mtshali, B Nair and C Ndlovu.

44 Interview, N Serache; and on that influence, see M Sparg, J Schreiner and G Ansell (eds), *Comrade Jack: The Political Lectures and Diary of Jack Simons, Novo Catengue* (Johannesburg, 2001).

45 Lodge, *Black Politics*, 75–6: Mandela, *Long Walk*, 136.

46 Interview, E Mtshali; Mgabela interview in Coetzee et al, *Fallen Walls*; A Sibeko (known in MK as Zola Zembe), *Freedom in Our Lifetime*. With J Leeson. (Durban, 1996), 49–50.

47 Interview, J Nkadimeng.

48 Confirmed by interview with Henry Makgothi.

49 Lodge, *Black Politics*, 75. See also Feit, *African Opposition*, 75.

50 Karis and Gerhart (eds), vol 3.

51 Mandela, *Long Walk*, 135–6; Lodge, *Black Politics*, 76.

52 B Bunting, *Moses Kotane: South African Revolutionary: A Political Biography*. 3rd ed. (Cape Town, 1998), 179.

53 Interview, E Mtshali.

54 Sampson, *Mandela*, 80; F Meli, *South Africa Belongs to Us: A History of the ANC* (Harare, Bloomington, London, 1988), 153; interviews, J Nkadimeng, E Mtshali, H Makgothi and N Setsubi.

55 Karis and Gerhart (eds), vol 3, 806.

56 Meli, *South Africa*, 153. This was not a formal national conference but a taking stock by all who could be there and as representative as security permitted at the time. Karis and Gerhart refer to it as the first 'ANC conference' since 1959, implying a higher level of authority than would appear to have been the case (Karis and Gerhart (eds), vol 3, 806).

57 Interview, Noloyiso Gasa.

58 Everatt, 'Politics of Nonracialism', 93; B Turok, *Nothing but the Truth: Behind the ANC's Struggle Politics* (Johannesburg, Cape Town, 2003), 53–4.

59 F Baard, *My Spirit Is Not Banned*. With B Schreiner. (Harare, 1986), 71.

60 D Massey, 'Who Would Not Have Been Aware?: The History of Fort Hare and Its Student Activists 1933–1973' (unpublished MA thesis, University of Fort Hare, Alice, 2001), 214.

61 G Mbeki, *The Struggle for Liberation in South Africa: A Short History* (Cape Town, 1992), 86.

62 Karis and Gerhart (eds), vol 3, 572.

63 M Dingake, *My Fight Against Apartheid* (London, 1987), 58–9.

64 Ibid.

65 J Frederikse, *The Unbreakable Thread: Non-racialism in South Africa* (Johannesburg, Harare, 1990), 93.

66 Dingake, *My Fight*, 58–9. See below for similar comments in Mtshali interview.

67 Interview, C Ndlovu.

68 The one who was not a member is Nelson Mandela. Some scholars have suggested informally that this is not true, but there is no public evidence to the contrary. The most significant recent public acknowledgement of membership is that of the late Walter Sisulu, who was at the time a member of the SACP Central Committee (see E Sisulu, *Walter and Albertina Sisulu*, 122, and W Sisulu, *I Will Go Singing*, 92).

69 Eric Mtshali expresses the view that it would not have succeeded without Communist Party involvement (interview), though A Kathrada (interview) argues that, while it would have been more difficult, the ANC would nevertheless have been able to establish itself underground.

70 Interview, E Mtshali.

71 Interviews, A Kathrada and B Bunting; A Lerumo (Michael Harmel), *Fifty Fighting Years: The South African Communist Party 1921–1971* (London, 1971), 88.

72 See Shubin, *ANC*.

73 Interview, E Mtshali.

74 Ibid.

75 Interviews, P Tshabalala and R Mgijima.

76 Interviews, J Matthews and C Ndlovu.

77 Phil Bonner believes, from research he has been conducting, that Matthews's point may well have validity (personal communication).

78 Dingake, *My Fight*, 68–9.

79 Ibid, 75–6.

80 Ibid, 77.

81 Ibid, 77–8.

82 Interview, S Mngqikana, and see Chapter 5.

83 Interview, S Mngqikana.

84 Interview, N Setsubi.

85 I van Kessel, *'Beyond Our Wildest Dreams': The United Democratic Front and the Transformation of South Africa* (Charlottesville VA, London, 2000).

CHAPTER 3

1 P Delius, *The Lion Amongst the Cattle: Reconstruction and Resistance in the Northern Transvaal* (Portsmouth NH, Johannesburg, Oxford, 1996) and personal information on Boshielo being a healer. S Johns, 'Invisible

Resurrection: The Recreation of a Communist Party in South Africa in the 1950s', *African Studies Quarterly* 9, 4 (Fall 2007), http://web.africa. ufl.edu/asq/v9i4a2.htm, reproduces this big city emphasis as well as a total reliance on written sources from such areas.

2 R Bernstein, *Memory Against Forgetting: Memoirs from a Life in South African Politics 1938–1964* (London, New York, 1999), 121.

3 Ibid, 123.

4 D Everatt, 'The Politics of Nonracialism: White Opposition to Apartheid 1945–1960' (unpublished DPhil thesis, Oxford University, 1990), 88, quoting interview with R Arenstein on concentration camps; J Simons and R Simons, *Class and Colour in South Africa 1850–1950* (London, 1983 [1969]), 607 on the German Communist experience.

5 Bernstein, *Memory*, 121–2.

6 Everatt, 'Politics of Nonracialism', quoting interview with R Bernstein, 89–90.

7 A Lerumo (Michael Harmel), *Fifty Fighting Years: The South African Communist Party 1921–1971* (London, 1971), 82.

8 Everatt, 'Politics of Nonracialism', 91; S Clingman, *Bram Fischer: Afrikaner Revolutionary* (Cape Town, Amherst MA, 1998), 188.

9 Everatt, 'Politics of Nonracialism', 91.

10 B Bunting, *Moses Kotane: South African Revolutionary: A Political Biography*. 3rd ed. (Cape Town, 1998), 179.

11 RA Simons, *All My Life and All My Strength*. Ed R Suttner. (Johannesburg, 2004), 276; Clingman, *Bram Fischer*, 207; I Meer, *A Fortunate Man* (Cape Town, 2002), 124.

12 Interview, B Nair.

13 Simons and Simons, *Class and Colour*, 276.

14 Interview, B Bunting.

15 Interview, A Kathrada.

16 Everatt, 'Politics of Nonracialism', 95ff.

17 Ibid.

18 South African Communist Party (SACP), *The Path to Power* (London, 1989), 19 and 18–32 generally; African National Congress (ANC), *Colonialism of a Special Type* (London, nd, c1980); P Jordan, 'The South African Liberation Movement and the Making of a New Nation' in M van Diepen (ed), *The National Question in South Africa* (London, New Jersey, 1988), 110–24.

19 Everatt, 'Politics of Nonracialism', 96.

20 Interview, B Bunting.

21 P Walshe, *The Rise of African Nationalism in South Africa: The African National Congress 1912–1952* (London, 1970), 389ff.

22 J Sanders, *Apartheid's Friends: The Rise and Fall of South Africa's Secret Service* (London, 2006).

23 M Meredith, *Fischer's Choice: A Life of Bram Fischer* (Johannesburg, Cape

Town, 2002), 42; see also J Slovo, *Slovo: The Unfinished Autobiography*. With introduction by Helena Dolny. (Johannesburg, London, 1995), 83–4.

24   Bunting, *Moses Kotane*, 197–198; interview, B Bunting.

25   Interview, A Kathrada.

26   Ibid. Berrangé may, according to some informants, have been a member before the Party's dissolution.

27   Interview, B Nair.

28   See also A Kathrada, interview.

29   B Magubane, P Bonner, J Sithole, P Delius, J Cherry, P Gibbs and T April, 'The Turn to Armed Struggle' in SADET, *Road to Democracy*, vol 1, 65.

30   Bunting, *Moses Kotane*, 236–7.

31   Interview, B Nair.

32   Interview, A Kathrada.

33   That Walter Sisulu's membership was only announced in the last years of his life indicates the type of sensitivity that Slovo tried to address. Given that Sisulu was Secretary-General (and after banning, *de facto* Secretary-General) of the ANC may have made his membership of the SACP a controversial and divisive question had it been announced in a predominantly anti-Communist world, even after his imprisonment.

34   Slovo, *Slovo*, 84.

35   In SACP, *South African Communists Speak* (London, 1981), 311.

36   Slovo, *Slovo*, 108.

37   Interview, J Matthews.

38   V Shubin, *ANC: A View from Moscow* (Cape Town, 1999), 332ff; P O'Malley, *Shades of Difference: Mac Maharaj and the Struggle for South Africa* (New York, 2007), 244–91, 353–6.

39   Interview, A Kathrada.

40   Interview, E Mtshali. See Delius, *The Lion*, 100 for a similar phenomenon in the Northern Transvaal.

41   Interview, J Matthews. V Shubin (personal communication, 29.9.2003) believes this is exaggeration.

42   Interview, A Kathrada.

43   B Turok, *Nothing but the Truth: Behind the ANC's Struggle Politics* (Johannesburg, Cape Town, 2004), 2.

44   Tom Lodge argues, however, that this was not simply a case of 'people' but an organisation within an organisation, deciding on a position and ensuring its implementation (personal communication, 11.5.2005).

45   Interview, B Nair.

46   Magubane et al, *Road to Democracy*, 54ff.

47   Karis and Gerhart (eds), *From Protest to Challenge*, vol 5: *Nadir and Resurgence 1964–1979* (Pretoria, 1997), 27.

48   Interview, P Mashatile.

49   Interview, R Potenza.

50 Shubin, *ANC*, 125.

51 See O'Malley, *Shades of Difference.*

52 Shubin, *ANC*, 14.

53 Magubane et al, *Road to Democracy*, 72ff.

54 See Bunting, *Moses Kotane.*

55 Shubin, *ANC*, 256–7, emphasis inserted.

56 Bunting, *Moses Kotane*, 236–7. If he thought this, Shubin points out, he was wrong because after 1950 (as we have noted), many communists did not join the underground Party (personal communication, 29.9.2003).

57 Bunting, 236–7, *Moses Kotane*, emphasis inserted.

58 Interview, D Mvelase.

59 Shubin believes that the answer to this question is 'both', that it differed from person to person and from time to time (personal communication, 29.9.2003).

60 Shubin, *ANC*, 112, and reservations of Slovo, *Slovo*, 112–13.

61 ANC, Green Book. Report of the Politico-Military Strategy Commission to the National Executive Committee, August 1979, 8–9. Housed in Karis-Gerhart papers, Cullen library, University of the Witwatersrand.

62 L Callinicos, *Oliver Tambo: Beyond the Engeli Mountains* (Cape Town, 2004), 526.

63 J Moleketi and J Jele, *Two Strategies of the National Liberation Movement in the Struggle for the Victory of the National Democratic Revolution* (Place of publication unstated, 2002).

64 N Mandela, *Long Walk to Freedom: The Autobiography of Nelson Mandela* (Johannesburg, 1994). Mandela erases from the history of struggle the fact that large numbers of African women were jailed in 1913 when they marched in Bloemfontein under the banner, 'We have done with pleading! We now demand!'; JC Wells, *We Now Demand!: The History of Women's Resistance to Pass Laws in South Africa* (Johannesburg, 1993); N Gasa, '"Let Them Build More Gaols"' in N.Gasa (ed), *Women in South African History* (Cape Town, 2007).

65 See Chapter 2 above.

CHAPTER 4

1 LM Thompson, *A History of South Africa* (New Haven, London, 2001), 211.

2 S Dubow, *The African National Congress* (Johannesburg, 2000), 7.

3 A Manson, B Mbenga and J Peires, 'The Afrikaner Nationalists in Power' in H Giliomee and B Mbenga (eds), *New History of South Africa* (Cape Town, 2007), 341.

4 M Dingake, *My Fight Against Apartheid* (London, 1987), 75.

5 SM Davis, *Apartheid's Rebels: Inside South Africa's Hidden War* (Johannesburg, 1987), 22.

6 TG Karis and GM Gerhart (eds), *From Protest to Challenge: A Documentary*

History of African Politics in South Africa 1882–1990, vol 5: *Nadir and Resurgence 1964–1979* (Pretoria, 1997), 29. See also N van Driel, 'The ANC's First Armed Military Operation: The Luthuli Detachment and the Wankie Campaign July–September 1967' (unpublished MA thesis, University of the Western Cape, 2003).

7   Interviews, L/T Dlamini, M Ngcobo and A Lengisi.

8   On the focus of the underground on sending people to join MK: Interview, A Qaba; E Sisulu, *Walter and Albertina Sisulu: In Our Lifetime* (Cape Town, 2002); and G Houston, 'Post-Rivonia ANC/SACP Underground' in South African Democratic Education Trust (SADET), *The Road to Democracy in South Africa*, vol 1: *1960–1970* (Cape Town, 2004) Chapter 15, 603ff. On the claim that the ANC failure to create the type of underground organisation that could sustain MK, see H Barrell, *MK: The ANC's Armed Struggle* (London, 1990) and H Barrell, 'Conscripts to Their Age: African National Congress Operational Strategy 1976–1986' (unpublished DPhil thesis, Oxford University, 1993).

9   See quotation from Joe Matthews in G Houston, 'Post-Rivonia', 372–3; personal communication from P Limb, 12.12.2002.

10 Nomboniso Gasa, 'Amandla: Songs of Life and the Struggle', *Sunday Independent*, 13.7.2003.

11 Interview, Noloyiso Gasa, reported on below.

12 Interviews with P Naidoo and Noloyiso Gasa. On this notion of unaffiliated illegal activity in support of the ANC, see also Houston, 'ANC Political Underground', 374ff.

13 See E Webster, 'A Profile of Unregistered Union Members in Durban', *South African Labour Bulletin* 48, 4 (1979), 51–2, 63–4 and E Webster 'Sociology in South Africa: Its Past, Present and Future', *Society in Transition* 35, 1 (2004), 31–2.

14 Houston, 'Post Rivonia', 603 and 617.

15 E Sisulu, *Walter and Albertina Sisulu*, 215.

16 Ibid; interview, B Manci.

17 E Sisulu, *Walter and Albertina Sisulu*, 215.

18 Houston, 'Post Rivonia', quoting interview with Dingake.

19 Ibid, 605–6, citing testimony of a state witness. This is stated as a fact by Houston, and from what emerges in E Sisulu it appears to be likely.

20 Ibid, 612–13.

21 Ibid, 645–6, note 208, citing interviews with Joyce Sikhakane and Nkadimeng.

22 Ibid.

23 Ibid, 647.

24 Personal communication from S Ndou, 9.1.2008.

25 Houston, 'Post Rivonia', 640.

26 Ibid, note 178.

27 Personal communication from J Daniel, 9.9.2004.

28 Houston, 'Post Rivonia', 641, citing interviews with Albertina Sisulu and John Nkadimeng

29 Ibid, citing interview with Themba (L) Dlamini; also my interview with him.

30 Houston, 'Post Rivonia', 643, citing interview with Lengisi; also my interviews with L Dlamini, A Lengisi and M Ngcobo.

31 Houston, 'Post Rivonia'.

32 Interviews, L Dlamini, A Lengisi and M Ngcobo as above.

33 F Buntman, *Robben Island and Prisoner Resistance to Apartheid* (Cambridge, 2003), 4, 20, 21, 149ff.

34 TC Moloi, 'Youth Politics: The Political Role of AZANYU in the Struggle for Liberation: The Case of AZANU Tembisa Branch, 1980s to 1996' (unpublished MA thesis, University of the Witwatersrand, 2005), 65ff; and Davis, *Apartheid's Rebels* (31–3) documents the role of Zeph Mothopeng in reconstructing a PAC cell in Krugersdorp in 1974.

35 Interview, H Makgothi. The concept of mandating prisoners on release was also true of the relatively small number of white political prisoners. See Marius Schoon, in J Frederikse, *The Unbreakable Thread: Non-racialism in South Africa* (Johannesburg, Harare, 1990), 151, and R Suttner, *Inside Apartheid's Prison* (Melbourne, New York, Pietermaritzburg, 2001), 109–10.

36 Interview, M Morobe.

37 Interviews, B Manci, J Nkadimeng and H Makgothi.

38 I Naidoo, *Island in Chains: Ten Years on Robben Island* (London, 2000), 268.

39 Frederikse, *The Unbreakable Thread*, 124.

40 Interview, P Gordhan.

41 Interviews, B Pityana and T Tryon.

42 T Karis and GM Gerhart (eds), *From Protest to Challenge: A Documentary History of African Politics in South Africa 1882–1964*, vol 3: *Challenge and Violence 1953–1964* (Stanford CA, 1977), 759–80.

43 Houston, 'Post-Rivonia', 612.

44 CD: Radio Freedom, Insert, *Voice of the African National Congress and the People's Army mKhonto weSizwe* (Place of publication unstated, 1996).

45 Houston, 'Post-Rivonia', 632ff.

46 Ibid, 635–6, quoting interview with Ronnie Kasrils.

47 See ibid, 635, note 157.

48 Ibid, 635.

49 In Frederikse, *The Unbreakable Thread*, 128.

50 Suttner, *Inside Apartheid's Prison*, Chapters 2 and 3.

51 This is not to say that every unit abided by such instructions. There was one I know of where both its white members were involved in relationships with black women while the Immorality Act, proscribing interracial sexual relations, was in force.

52 See Suttner, *Inside Apartheid's Prison*, Chapters 2 and 3.

53 Ibid; M Legassick, *Armed Struggle and Democracy: The Case of South Africa* (Uppsala, 2002), 31. See also interview with Setsubi below.

54 L Callinicos, *Oliver Tambo: Beyond the Engeli Mountains* (Cape Town, 2004), 387. This example may have been in the period slightly after 1976.

55 Interview, P Naidoo.

56 A Sibeko [R Kasrils], 'The Underground Voice' in A Mattelart and S Siegelaub (eds), *Communication and Class struggle*, vol 2 (New York, 1983 [1977]), 206.

57 See A Manson, *The Troubles of Chief Abram Moilwa: The Hurutshe Resistance of 1954–1958* (Johannesburg, 1983) and A Manson, 'The Hurutshe Resistance in Zeerust 1954–1959', *Africa Perspective* 22 (1983), 62–79.

58 J Fairbairn, 'Zeerust: A Profile of Resistance', *Africa South* 2, 3 (1958), 31.

59 Interview, V Moche.

60 Ibid, on the reference to the tree.

61 Interview, Noloyiso Gasa.

62 Ibid.

63 See LK von den Steinen, 'Soldiers in the Struggle: Aspects of the Experiences of mKhonto weSizwe's Rank and File Soldiers – The Soweto Generation and After' (unpublished MA thesis, University of Cape Town, 1999), 59–60.

64 Interviews, N Setsubi and M Mandubu.

65 Interview, N Setsubi.

66 In Frederikse, *The Unbreakable Thread*, 157–9.

67 *State v Sexwale*, statements of Sexwale. Record provided by the late Raymond Tucker, attorney.

68 Interview, 'A'.

69 See Frederikse, *The Unbreakable Thread*, 110, for interview with Masterpiece Gumede, and AW Marx, *Lessons of Struggle: South African Internal Opposition 1960–1990* (Cape Town, 1992), 250. See also Karis and Gerhart (eds), vol 5, 97–8.

70 Interview, R Mgijima.

71 Interview, B Pityana.

72 E Sisulu, *Walter and Albertina Sisulu*, 235

73 In Frederikse, *The Unbreakable Thread*, 115. Interview, A Masondo, has similar sentiments.

74 Interviews, B Pityana, M Morobe and R Mgijima.

75 Frederikse, *The Unbreakable Thread*, 114; interview, R Mgijima.

76 E Sisulu, *Walter and Albertina Sisulu*, 235. For a more qualified response, see N Mandela, 'Whither the Black Consciousness Movement? An Assessment' in M Maharaj (ed), *Reflections in Prison* (Cape Town, 2001), 21ff.

77 On Robben Island, see Buntman *Robben Island*; interview, A Masondo.

78 Interview, B Pityana.

79 Interview, N Serache.

80 Also Morobe interview.

81 Barney Pityana did have some contact with him, of which Serache may have been unaware (Pityana interview).

82 E Sisulu, *Walter and Albertina Sisulu*, 235; DVD *A South African Love Story: Walter and Albertina Sisulu*. Directed by T Strasburg. (Quest Star Communication, 2004); and see below.

83 To this day the Black Consciousness trend remains very highly represented in the country's media and also academia.

84 Marx, *Lessons of Struggle*, 100.

85 Frederikse, *The Unbreakable Thread*, 110.

86 Interview, R Mgijima.

87 A similar review is required for the 1973 Natal strikes.

88 Interview, P Tshabalala, regarding the direct role of Albertina Sisulu.

89 Von den Steinen, 'Soldiers in the Struggle', 51.

90 Interview, Mgijima.

91 Interview, B Pityana.

92 Interview, Paul Mashatile, though this relates to the 1980s.

CHAPTER 5

1 Helen Bradford, email of 7.6.2004, has pointed to the fact that all the potential sources of danger to the operative were depicted as being female.

2 See General H Stadler, quoted in Karis and Gerhart (ed), *From Protest to Challenge*, vol 5: *Nadir and Resurgence 1964–1979* (Pretoria, 1997), 24.

3 Interview, L Dlamini.

4 Interview, Z Jaffer; and Z Jaffer, *Our Generation* (Cape Town, 2003).

5 Interview, L Dlamini.

6 Interview, General S Shoke, now Chief of the South African National Defence Force.

7 N van Driel, 'The ANC's First Armed Military Operation: The Luthuli Detachment and the Wankie Campaign July–September 1967' (unpublished MA thesis, University of the Western Cape, 2003) and personal communication, 28.6.2004.

8 Personal communication from Dr L Piper, 8.9.2005, on basis of his research with a former Security Policeman.

9 The depoliticisation could also be manifested if arrested and appearing in court, where some people who had been highly proficient in committing acts of sabotage or issuing inflammatory pamphlets were sometimes prepared to follow legal advice and make submissions which amounted to renunciation of their political beliefs. The professional interventions of lawyers changed over time, with many of the lawyers of the 1980s themselves being activists. But the lawyers wanted to do their best for

their clients *as individuals*. This sometimes created a conflict between the possibility of securing release from detention or serving a sentence and the needs of the organisation, which may have required refusing to make a particular category of statement. In writing this, I am aware that it reveals my own acceptance of the notion of supremacy of the collective or organisational needs over that of the individual in the conditions then prevailing. For discussion of this paradigm in other contexts, see below in this chapter.

10 See R Suttner, *Inside Apartheid's Prison* (Melbourne, New York, Pietermaritzburg, 2001), 16–17 and elsewhere.

11 Personal communication, R Kasrils, during training in 1970.

12 Interview, E Mtshali.

13 Interviews, R Potenza, R Mgijima, E Mtshali, C Ndlovu and F Mohlala.

14 Interviews, N Serache, P Jordan, F Radebe and T Memela.

15 Interview, P 'Shoes' Mashigo.

16 Interview, S Shoke; G Houston and B Magubane, 'The ANC's Armed Struggle in the 1970s' in South African Democratic Education Trust (SADET), *The Road to Democracy*, vol 2, *1970–1980* (Pretoria, 2006), 463.

17 VI Lenin, 'What Is to Be Done? Burning Questions of Our Movement' in VI Lenin, *Selected Works in Three Volumes*, vol 1 (Moscow, 1977 [1902]).

18 N Harding, *Lenin's Political Thought: Theory and Practice in the Democratic and Socialist Revolution* (London, 1983), vol 1, 50 and more generally 49–54, citing in translation works published in Russian.

19 A Davidson, I Filatova, V Gorodnov and S Johns (eds), *The Communist International and South Africa: Documentary History 1919–1939*, vol 1 (London, 2003), 76.

20 See also the broader lineage found in writings of C Guevara, *Che Guevara Reader: Writings on Guerrilla Strategy, Politics and Revolution*. Ed. D Deutschmann. (Melbourne, New York, 1997 [1965]), 198.

21 This point has been indirectly suggested to me by Michael Neocosmos.

22 See interviews with Nat Serache on the role of Joe Gqabi in Chapter 4; interview, General P Mothupi; G Houston, 'The ANC/SACP Underground in the 1970s' in SADET, vol 2: *1970–1980* (Pretoria, 2006), Chapter 8.

23 S Binda, 'Notes on the Life of Comrade Chris Hani' (unpublished, 1993), 2.

24 For example, interview, L Dlamini.

25 See A Sparks, *The Mind of South Africa: The Story of the Rise and Fall of Apartheid* (London, 1990), 242.

26 Interview, P Tshabalala.

27 Suttner, *Inside Apartheid's Prison*, Chapters 2 and 3.

28 Interview, F Mohlala.

29 Ibid.

30 Documentation obtained through these channels has been provided to the Hefer Commission. I had some knowledge of this through association with people operating in the Natal area in the 1980s.

31 I do not elaborate on this matter because I conducted this interview some years ago and have not had the opportunity to discuss with the individual concerned on whether or when to make the matter public, and how.

CHAPTER 6

1 See P Walshe, *The Rise of African Nationalism in South Africa: The African National Congress 1912–1952* (London, 1970); F Meli, *South Africa Belongs to Us: A History of the ANC* (Harare, Bloomington, London, 1988); S Dubow, *The African National Congress* (Johannesburg, 2000).

2 See C Walker, *Women and Resistance in South Africa*. 2nd ed. (Cape Town, Johannesburg, New York, 1991); JC Wells, *We Now Demand!: The History of Women's Resistance to Pass Laws in South Africa* (Johannesburg, 1993); S Hassim, *Women's Organizations and Democracy in South Africa: Contesting Authority* (Scottsville, 2006); N Gasa (ed), *Women in South African History* (Cape Town, 2007).

3 See Democratic Education Trust (SADET), *The Road to Democracy in South Africa*, vol 1: *1960–1970* (Cape Town, 2004) and vol 2: *1970–1980* (Pretoria, 2006); and E Feit, *African Opposition in South Africa: The Failure of Passive Resistance* (Stanford CA, 1967).

4 Personal communications from certain leading scholars.

5 E Unterhalter, '"The Work of the Nation": Heroic Masculinity in South African Autobiographical Writing of the Anti-apartheid Struggle', *European Journal of Development Research* 12, 2 (2000), 167–72, referring to Joe Slovo's autobiography *Slovo*.

6 Personal communication, Nomboniso Gasa, 20.12.2007.

7 Hassim, *Women's Organizations*, Chapter 3, makes little distinction between the differing ethos within various facets of exile and the military itself, where conditions were significantly different.

8 See S Walby, *Gender Transformations* (London, New York, 1997), 6–7, 9, 11–12, 172 and 178.

9 Quoting S Johns III, in S Johns III (ed), *From Protest to Challenge: A Documentary History of African Politics in South Africa 1882–1964*, vol 1: *Protest and Hope 1882–1934* (Stanford, 1972), 317.

10 Citing 'Bantu and Politics,' c1935, AD 843, Xuma Papers, Box O, Department of Historical Papers, University of the Witwatersrand.

11 N Erlank, 'Gender and Masculinity in South African Nationalist Discourse 1912–1950', *Feminist Studies* 29 (2003), 653. Emphasis inserted.

12 Interestingly, British construction of Indian men, especially in Bengal, was to depict them as effeminate and physically weak. See I Chowdhury, *The Frail Hero and Virile History: Gender and the Politics of Culture in Colonial Bengal* (Delhi, 1998); and M Sinha, *Colonial Masculinity: The*

'*Manly Englishman*' *and the* '*Effeminate Bengali*' *in the Late Nineteenth Century* (New Delhi, 1997).

13 In M Morris, *Every Step of the Way: The Journey to Freedom in South Africa* (Cape Town, 2004), 152.

14 See HJ Simons, *African Women: Their Legal Status in South Africa* (London, 1968), 15.

15 Captured well in regard to European depiction of the Chinese by Joseph Needham, *Within the Four Seas: The Dialogue of East and West* (London, 1969), 13.

16 See D Welsh, *The Roots of Segregation: Native Policy in Colonial Natal 1845–1910* (Cape Town, New York, 1971) and M Mamdani, *Citizen and Subject: Contemporary Africa and the Legacy of Late Colonialism* (Princeton, 1996).

17 J Iliffe, *Honour in African Society* (Cambridge, 2005), 3.

18 As seen in Walby, this is true, though not in quite the same way in a range of spheres.

19 See Simons, *African Women* and Welsh, *Roots of Segregation*.

20 Interview, M Ngcobo.

21 Personal communication, Nomboniso Gasa.

22 J Tosh, *Manliness and Masculinities in Nineteenth-Century Britain: Essays on Gender, Family and Empire* (Edinburgh, 2005), 5.

23 Erlank, 'Gender', 652–3. See above.

24 See N Gasa, '"Let Them Build More Gaols"' in N Gasa (ed), *Women in South African History* (Cape Town, 2007), 129–52.

25 See F Ginwala, 'Women and the African National Congress 1912–1943', *Agenda* 8 (1990), 77–93.

26 J Frederikse, *The Unbreakable Thread: Non-racialism in South Africa* (Johannesburg, Harare, 1990), 158. Emphasis inserted.

27 P Delius, *A Lion Amongst the Cattle* (Johannesburg, Oxford, 1996), 129.

28 Interview, Z Nkondo.

29 Reflecting that such concerns were not baseless, a rape of a young girl resulting from police arrest for passes is reported by C Hooper, *Brief Authority* (Cape Town, 1989 [1960]), 10.

30 The number is approximate because some of the original eighty were sent back by the then Bechuanaland authorities.

31 Interview, RJ Moumakwa.

32 E-mail, PM Sebate, 20.5.2003.

33 From CD by Radio Freedom, *Voice of the African National Congress and the People's Army mKhonto weSizwe* (Cambridge, 1996).

34 See J Peteet, 'Male Gender and Rituals of Resistance in the Palestinian Intifada' in R Adams and D Safran (eds), *The Masculinity Studies Reader* (Malden, Oxford, 2002), Chapter 18.

35 Interview, M Mandubu.

36 S Morrow, B Maaba and L Pulumani, *Education in Exile: SOMAFCO, the ANC School in Exile* (Cape Town, 2004), 107.

37 Interview in JK Coetzee, L Gilfillan and O Hulec (eds), *Fallen Walls: Voices from the Cells that Held Mandela and Havel* (Cape Town, 2002). One white warder was also circumcised by him.

38 See P Mayer, '"Traditional" Manhood Initiation in an Industrial City: The African View' in EJ de Jager (ed), *Man: Anthropological Essays Presented to OF Raum* (Cape Town, 1971), 7–18.

39 Interview, A Lengisi, who was underground, in exile, and in prison.

40 Unterhalter, '"The Work of the Nation"', 158, 163ff.

41 J Fucik, *Report from the Gallows* (Prague, 1951).

42 See J Guy, *Remembering the Rebellion: The Zulu Uprising of 1906* (Scottsville, 2006).

43 See JC Wells, *Rebellion and Uproar: Makhanda and the Great Escape from Robben Island 1820* (Pretoria, 2007).

44 T Pringle, *Narrative of a Residence in South Africa* (Cape Town, 1996 [1824]) 285–7.

45 J Weir, 'Chiefly Women and Women's Leadership in Pre-colonial Southern Africa' in Gasa (ed), *Women*, Chapter 3.

46 A Sampson, *Mandela: The Authorised Biography* (London, 1999), 196. It should be recognised, as indicated earlier, that such an affirmation of manliness in the context of apartheid is simultaneously an assertion of human personhood, a claim for dignity.

47 LH Keeley, *War before Civilization* (New York, Oxford, 1996), 86. See also C Cockburn, *The Space Between Us: Negotiating Gender and Identities in Conflict* (London, New York, 1998), 222–3.

48 See, for example, G Harinck, 'Interaction between Xhosa and Khoi: Emphasis on the Period 1620–1750' in L Thompson (ed), *African Societies in Southern Africa* (London, Ibadan, Nairobi, 1969) and JB Peires, *The House of Phalo: A History of the Xhosa People in the Days of Their Independence* (Johannesburg, 1981), 19.

49 See M Motsei, *The Kanga and the Kangaroo Court* (Johannesburg, 2007), 104ff.

50 A A Mazrui, 'Manhood, Warriorhood and Sex in Eastern Africa' in A A Mazrui (ed), *The Warrior Tradition in Modern Africa* (Leiden, 1977), 74.

51 See Cockburn, *Space Between Us*, for example.

52 Unterhalter, '"The Work of the Nation"', 166.

53 Interview, W Sisulu.

54 E-mail, E Unterhalter, 13.12.2007.

55 Unterhalter, '"The Work of the Nation"', 166–7.

56 B Turok, *Nothing but the Truth: Behind the ANC's Struggle Politics* (Johannesburg, Cape Town, 2003), 130. Emphasis inserted.

57 See below and interview, F Radebe.

58 See RA Simons, *All My Life and All My Strength*. Ed R Suttner. (Johannesburg, 2004), and see Chapter 3.

59 Ibid.

60 K Luckhardt and B Wall, *Organise or Starve!: The History of the South African Congress of Trade Unions* (London, 1980), 177–8, who refer to Mini as a 'musician and poet of exceptional quality'. See also 'Vuyisile Mini: Worker, Poet and Martyr for Freedom' (nd), 6, http://www.anc.org.za/ancdocs/history/misc/mini.html, and V Mini (nd, c1986), http://www.sacp.org.za/biographies/vmini.html.

61 He was also to die after torture in police detention.

62 Interview, S Mngqikana.

63 See S Whitehead, *Men and Masculinities* (Cambridge, 2002), Chapter 5 esp 179, and RW Connell, *Masculinities*. 2nd ed. (Cambridge, 2005) 39, 164–5, 187.

64 Interview, F Radebe.

65 JC Wells, 'The Rise and Fall of Motherism as a Force in Black Women's Resistance Movements' in *Conference on Women and Gender in Southern Africa* (Durban, 1990).

66 A dead letter box is a place where an agent can hide arms or other incriminating items for collection by another agent later.

67 Interview, T Memela.

68 J Cock, *Colonels and Cadres: War and Gender in South Africa* (Oxford, Cape Town, 1991), 162.

69 Gwendoline Sello, in H Bernstein, *The Rift: The Exile Experience of South Africans* (London, 1994), 149. See also Cock, *Colonels and Cadres*, esp Chapter 5, and Jacqueline Molefe in Cock, 164.

70 Hassim, *Women's Organizations*, Chapter 3, appears to make no allowance for or else to be unaware of these divergences in response on the part of men.

71 Interview, D Mvelase.

72 See Sello in Bernstein, *The Rift*, 149 and LK von den Steinen, 'Soldiers in the Struggle: Aspects of the Experiences of umKhonto weSizwe's Rank and File Soldiers – the Soweto Generation and After' (unpublished MA thesis, University of Cape Town, 1999), 191–2. See also Modise interview in R Curnow, 'Interview: Thandi Modise, a Woman at War', *Agenda* 43 (2000), 39.

73 Personal communication, Nomboniso Gasa, 1.1.2008.

74 T Mtintso, 'Women in MK' interview with D Pillay, *Work in Progress* 80 (1992), 18.

75 Interview, S Gunn.

76 See T Modise, in Cock, *Colonels and Cadres*, 151 for a different statement of experience. Modise's account in Curnow is less positive and, being later, less likely to be influenced by disciplinary constraints.

77 See Cock, *Colonels and Cadres*, 163.

78 Interview, F Radebe.

79 Von den Steinen, 'Soldiers in the Struggle', 196–7.

80 Interview, D Mvelase.
81 Von den Steinen, 'Soldiers in the Struggle', 205ff.
82 Hassim, *Women's Organizations*, 89.
83 Ibid.
84 Interview, Radebe.
85 Von den Steinen, 'Soldiers in the Struggle', 206. Interview with Gunn, who took her baby with her when conducting reconnaissance.
86 For example, the Radebe interview.
87 L Mashike, '"Some of Us Know Nothing Except Military Skills": South Africa's Former Guerrilla Combatants' in S Buhlungu, J Daniel, R Southall and J Lutchman (eds), *State of the Nation: South Africa 2007* (Cape Town, 2007), 367.
88 Ibid. See also Motsei.
89 Cock, *Colonels and Cadres*, 168.
90 See, for example, RW Connell, *The Men and the Boys* (Berkeley CA, 2000), 16–17.
91 M Randall, *Women Brave in the Face of Danger: Photographs and Writings by Latin and North American Women* (New York, 1985), unnumbered page.

CHAPTER 7

1 See N Saifulin and P Dixon, *Soviet Dictionary of Philosophy* (Moscow, 1984), 73–4, and H Aptheker, *The Urgent Necessity of a Marxist–Christian Diaologue* (New York, 1971).
2 Respectively, assassinated Communist leader, Communist leader who died while serving a life sentence for sabotage, and liberation movement and Communist intellectual murdered by a parcel bomb in Maputo. See T Mali, *Tami Mali Remembers Chris Hani: The Sun Before Dawn* (Johannesburg, 1993); M Berger, *Chris Hani* (Cape Town, 1993); S Clingman, *Bram Fischer: Afrikaner Revolutionary* (Cape Town, Amherst MA, 1998) and D Pinnock, *Writing Left: The Radical Journalism of Ruth First* (Pretoria, 2007).
3 See E Sisulu, *Walter and Albertina Sisulu: In Our Lifetime* (Cape Town, 2002) and R Suttner, 'A Revolutionary Love', *Mail & Guardian*, 19.2.2003.
4 See EH Carr, *The Bolshevik Revolution*, vol 1 (Harmondsworth, 1966 [1950]).
5 B Turok, *Nothing but the Truth: Behind the ANC's Struggle Politics* (Johannesburg, Cape Town, 2003), 234.
6 Ibid.
7 Interview, B Bunting.
8 See discussion in R Suttner, 'Being a Revolutionary: Reincarnation or Carrying over Previous Identities? A Review Article', *Social Identities* 10 (2004), 415–31.

9 See R Suttner, 'The Jacob Zuma Rape Trial: Power and ANC Masculinities' forthcoming in V Reddy, C Potgieter and P Gqola (eds), (Title undecided) (Cape Town, 2008).

10 An early attempt to analyse this, which has become dated in a very few months, is R Suttner, 'African National Congress (ANC): Attainment of Power, Post-Liberation Phases and Current Crisis', *Historia* 52, 1 (2007), 1–46.

11 I do not refer to centralisation in the ANC, which I believe is a myth in that government has taken the decision, purporting to act on behalf of the ANC, whether or not the thinking has passed through organisational structures on matters such as macroeconomic policies. There is now a tension since the ANC elections of December 2007, with ANC and state presidents being two different individuals, which could lead to some degree of shift.

12 N Mandela, *Long Walk to Freedom: The Autobiography of Nelson Mandela* (Johannesburg, 1994), 347

13 Liu, Shao Qi, *Selected Works*, vol 1 (Beijing, 1984 [1939]), 136–7. Capitals in original.

14 See G Hermet, *The Communists in Spain: A Study of an Underground Political Movement* (Westmeath (Hants), 1971), 148ff.

15 C Guevara, *Che Guevara Reader: Writings on Guerrilla Strategy, Politics and Revolution*. Ed. D Deutschmann. (Melbourne, New York, 1997 [1965]), 211–12.

16 See examples in many of the interviews in H Bernstein, *The Rift: The Exile Experience of South Africans* (London, 1994).

17 WB Yeats, *The Collected Poems of WB Yeats* (London and Basingstoke, 1973 [2nd ed 1950]), 204.

18 This numbing of the emotions was also very necessary in prison, where prisoners sometimes felt that allowing themselves to hope for release and a satisfying personal life – especially when in indefinite detention – would weaken their resolve. See Suttner, *Inside Apartheid's Prison* (Melbourne, New York, Pietermaritzburg, 2001).

19 For example, N Duka, *From Shantytown to Forest: The Story of Norman Duka*. Ed. D Mercer and G Mercer. (Richmond BC, 1974), 58ff; T Nkobi in Bernstein, *The Rift*, 16–17; Ruth Mompati in Bernstein, 18–20, 21–22.

20 Interview, E Mtshali, and supplementary personal communication from J Sithole. See also L Callinicos, *Oliver Tambo: Beyond the Engeli Mountains* (Cape Town, 2004), for similar examples.

21 Apart from the earlier quotation regarding sacrifices that the revolution demanded from families of the leaders, one of the most famous revolutionary statements, Che Guevara's farewell letter to Fidel Castro in resigning from the Cuban government, includes the remark: 'Wherever I am, I will feel the responsibility of being a Cuban revolutionary, and I shall behave as such. *I am not ashamed that I leave nothing material to my*

children and my wife: I am happy it is that way. I ask nothing for them, as the state will provide them with enough to live on and have an education' (Guevara, 354. Emphasis inserted). It should be noted that in this case, as is evident from utterances of the Guevara family, they bore no resentment for the decisions Che Guevara took which impacted on their lives. See quotation from Aleida Guevara below.

22 Interview, I Maphotho. Maphoto was one of a number of South Africans who spent more than ten years in Rhodesian jails after being captured in the Wankie or Sipolilo campaigns – a part of resistance history that still needs to be adequately documented.

23 Interview, A Qaba.

24 Bernstein, *The Rift*, xiv.

25 Ibid, 20.

26 Ibid, 21–2, and also her interview with Thuso Mashaba, at 67, 70, 71.

27 E Sisulu, *Walter and Albertina Sisulu*, and Suttner, 'A Revolutionary Love'.

28 See DVD *A South African Love Story: Walter and Albertina Sisulu*. Directed by T Strasburg. (Quest Star Communication, 2004).

29 The testimony of Guevara's daughter Aleida, in an article on his *Motor Cycle Diaries*, indicates an atmosphere of love in the family environment. See 'Riding My Father's Motorcycle' at http://www.cubasolidarity.com/aboutcuba/cubaspeaks/cheguevara/041009aleida.htm, where she describes him as 'the most complete man I've ever met'.

30 Guevara, *Che Guevara Reader*, 211–12. See similar sentiments in Liu Shao Qi, *Selected Works*, 137.

31 RA Simons, *All My Life and All My Strength*. Ed R Suttner. (Johannesburg, 2004), 81. Italics inserted. For a similar sentiment see the poem 'Girl of the Sandinista Front' in M Randall, *Sandino's Daughters: Testimonies of Nicaraguan Women in Struggle*. Ed. L Yanz. (London, Vancouver, Toronto, 1981) 129.

32 Hermet, *Communists in Spain*, 149.

33 G Frankel, *Rivonia's Children: Three Families and the Price of Freedom on South Africa* (Johannesburg, 1999), 58. Also interview, L Dlamini, on the words used in being recruited.

34 In Z Majodina, *Exiles and Homecoming: The Untold Stories* (Johannesburg, 1995), 29. See also Callinicos, *Oliver Tambo*, 416–7 and 429; and see comments on Hassim's work in Chapter 6 above.

35 R Suttner and J Cronin, *Fifty Years of the Freedom Charter* (Pretoria, 2006), 12; LK von den Steinen, 'Soldiers in the Struggle: Aspects of the Experiences of mKhonto we Sizwe's Rank and File Soldiers – The Soweto Generation and After' (unpublished MA thesis, University of Cape Town, 1999), 207–8.

36 Ibid, 207.

37 Interviews, B Mbete and P Jordan.

38 Interview, P Tshabalala, confirmed by interview, F Radebe; FG Reddy and SM Karterud, '"Must the Revolution Eat Its Children?": Working with the African National Congress (ANC) in Exile and Following Its Return' in MF Ettlin, JW Fidler and BD Cohen (eds), *Group Process and Political Dynamics* (New York, 1995), 227.

39 S Hassim, *Women's Organizations and Democracy in South Africa: Contesting Authority* (Scottsville, 2006), 88–89.

40 Interview, N Setsubi, reports similar impressions.

41 Interview, D Mvelase.

42 Ibid.

43 Reddy and Karterud, '"Must the Revolution Eat Its Children"', 226. Italics inserted.

CHAPTER 8

1 In JK Coetzee, L Gilfillan and O Hulec (eds), *Fallen Walls: Voices from the Cells that Held Mandela and Havel* (Cape Town, 2002), 35.

2 Interviews, Gunn and Jaffer.

3 See P Walshe, *The Rise of African Nationalism in South Africa: The African National Congress 1912–1952* (London, 1970). This is qualified by research published in P Limb, '"I-Kongilesi Lilizwi ezindi ezindliwini (Congress Name Is Household)": Politics and Class in the Cape Province during the 1920s', *Historia* 51 (2006), 49–86.

4 Interview with P Delius, *A Lion Amongst the Cattle* (Johannesburg, Oxford, 1996), 101.

5 T Karis and GM Gerhart (eds), *From Protest to Challenge: A Documentary History of African Politics in South Africa 1882–1964*, vol 5: *Nadir and Resurgence 1964–1979* (Pretoria, 1997), 326ff.

6 See R Suttner, 'Transformation of Political Parties in Africa Today', *Transformation* 55 (2004), 1–27.

7 For a general overview and new introductory reflection on the difference between debates of the 1980s and today, see R Suttner and J Cronin, *Fifty Years of the Freedom Charter* (Pretoria, 2006).

8 S Buhlungu, 'Rebels without a Cause of Their Own?: The Contradictory Location of White Officials in Black Unions in South Africa 1973–1994', *Current Sociology* 54 (2006), 427–51.

9 How much of this comment still holds at the time of writing, with Zuma just having defeated Mbeki in ANC elections in December 2007, remains to be seen. This reference is mainly to the pre-Zuma dismissal period, where such norms were in operation and represented a consensus amongst an as yet undivided ANC in government. My guess is that there will not be substantial ideological differences between a future Zuma government (if he becomes State President) and an Mbeki one.

10 R Edgar, 'Changing the Old Guard: AP Mda and the ANC Youth League 1944–1949' in S Dubow and A Jeeves (eds), *South Africa's 1940s: Worlds of*

Possibilities (Cape Town, 2005), 149 and 165–166.

11 R Suttner, 'Culture(s) of the ANC of South Africa: Imprint of Exile Experiences', *Journal of Contemporary African Studies* 21 (2003), 303–20; Interviews with N Serache and F Radebe.

12 Interview, F Radebe; L Callinicos, *Oliver Tambo: Beyond the Engeli Mountains* (Cape Town, 2004), 435.

13 Mzala, *Gatsha Buthelezi: Chief with a Double Agenda* (London, New Jersey, 1988).

14 R Suttner, 'The Formation and Functioning of Intellectuals Within the ANC-Led Liberation Movement' in T Mkandawire (ed), *African Intellectuals* (Dakar, London, 2005).

15 See ANC, Green Book. Report of the Politico-Military Strategy Commission to the National Executive Committee, August 1979. Housed in Karis-Gerhart papers, Cullen library, University of the Witwatersrand; and ANC, 'Strategy and Tactics of the ANC', 1969, www.anc.org.za/history/stratact.html.

16 M Sparg, J Schreiner and G Ansell (eds), *Comrade Jack: The Political Lectures and Diary of Jack Simons: Novo Catengue* (Johannesburg, 2001); interview, N Serache.

17 Interview, Memela.

18 ANC, 'Strategy and Tactics'.

19 Interview, M Ngcobo.

20 A Gramsci, *Selections from the Prison Notebooks*. Ed Q Hoare and G Nowell Smith. (London, 1971), 238–9.

21 Karis and Gerhart (eds), *From Protest to Challenge*, vol. 5, xxi.

22 Similar phrases in ibid are found on 6 and 181 (while on that same page presenting evidence showing its internal, underground existence).

INDEX

ABOUT THE BOOK

It is widely assumed that the African National Congress essentially disappeared from South Africa after its banning in 1960 and the imprisonment of its leaders, until public support for it revived in the wake of the 1976 Soweto uprising. Raymond Suttner takes issue with that view.

Drawing on extensive oral testimony, Suttner reveals how internally based activists, often working independently of the ANC in exile, were able to reconstitute and maintain effective underground networks. His scope encompasses the broad features of the clandestine work, the impact that it had on personal lives and the opportunities that were presented for both bravery and abuse. He also considers the gendered character of the underground ANC. In the concluding chapter of the book, he explores the gradual establishment of the ANC hegemony, which continues to this day.

Raymond Suttner is professor and head of the Walter and Albertina Sisulu Knowledge and Heritage Unit, School for Graduate Studies, University of South Africa. During the apartheid era, he was jailed for his activities as an ANC underground operative, an experience described in one of his earlier books, *Inside Apartheid's Prison*.